"In a permissive culture that l[...] confused about discipline, this [...] ing parents that discipline is a critical element of parental love, but also showing parents how to practically discipline their children in a way that is consistent, God honoring, and productive."

Paul David Tripp, President, Paul Tripp Ministries; author, *Parenting: 14 Gospel Principles That Can Radically Change Your Family*

"My wife and I were fortunate to attend a seminar on parenting young children featuring Sam Crabtree. He revealed the inconsistency and lack of logic often found in parenting young children and offered better alternatives. We were fortunate because we were able to take his wisdom and apply it to our children at just the right time. I have no doubt that many (if not all) parents experience the same sort of exasperation we did with our first child. And I have no doubt they will find Sam's wisdom in *Parenting with Loving Correction* as helpful as we did."

Paul K. Lim, MD, Trustee, Bethlehem College and Seminary; surgeon

"When my wife and I read this book, we immediately saw its value and wanted others to read it, so I was pleased when our small group agreed to go through it. But I was also a bit nervous—would the subject of parental discipline create conflict during group discussions because of differing parenting styles? Would the concept of correction (which is often considered in our culture to be overly negative) result in gloomy conversations? I needn't have worried. Sam Crabtree uses definitions, Scripture, and helpful anecdotes to get everyone on the same page. His pastoral heart is shown in each chapter as he writes with care, grace, and humility. I can tell you from personal experience that this book yields fruitful discussion—and parenting. Chapter 3 ends with this statement: 'There is great hope. And there is help.' For the believing parent, there is. And you will find both in this book."

Scott Jamison, small group leader

"As parents, it can seem like we're constantly training, correcting, and disciplining our children. Thankfully, Sam Crabtree has given us a gospel-infused framework for the kind of loving correction that will help all of us train up a child in the way he or she should go."

Bob Lepine, Cohost, *FamilyLife Today*; Pastor, Redeemer Community Church, Little Rock, Arkansas

Parenting with
Loving Correction

Parenting
with
Loving
Correction

Practical Help for
Raising Young Children

Sam Crabtree

:: CROSSWAY®
WHEATON, ILLINOIS

Parenting with Loving Correction: Practical Help for Raising Young Children

Copyright © 2019 by Sam Crabtree

Published by Crossway
        1300 Crescent Street
        Wheaton, Illinois 60187

Cover image and design: Derek Thornton, Faceout Studios

First printing 2018

Printed in the United States of America

Unless otherwise indicated, Scripture quotations are from the ESV® Bible (The Holy Bible, English Standard Version®), copyright © 2001 by Crossway, a publishing ministry of Good News Publishers. Used by permission. All rights reserved.

Scripture quotations marked HCSB have been taken from *The Holman Christian Standard Bible*®. Copyright © 1999, 2000, 2002, 2003 by Holman Bible Publishers. Used by permission.

All emphases in Scripture quotations have been added by the author.

Trade paperback ISBN: 978-1-4335-6061-3
ePub ISBN: 978-1-4335-6064-4
PDF ISBN: 978-1-4335-6062-0
Mobipocket ISBN: 978-1-4335-6063-7

Library of Congress Cataloging-in-Publication Data

Names: Crabtree, Sam, 1950– author.
Title: Parenting with loving correction : practical help for raising young children / Sam Crabtree.
Description: Wheaton, Illinois : Crossway, [2019] | Includes bibliographical references and index.
Identifiers: LCCN 2018021695 (print) | LCCN 2018041958 (ebook) | ISBN 9781433560620 (pdf)
    | ISBN 9781433560637 (mobi) | ISBN 9781433560644 (epub) | ISBN 9781433560613 (trade
    paperback) | ISBN 9781433560644 (epub) | ISBN 9781433560637 (mobipocket)
Subjects: LCSH: Parenting—Religious aspects—Christianity. | Child rearing—Religious aspects—
    Christianity. | Discipline of children—Religious aspects—Christianity.
Classification: LCC BV4529 (ebook) | LCC BV4529 .C73 2019 (print) | DDC 248.8/45—dc23
LC record available at https://lccn.loc.gov/2018021695

Crossway is a publishing ministry of Good News Publishers.

LB		29	28	27	26	25	24	23	22	21	20	19
15	14	13	12	11	10	9	8	7	6	5	4	3	2	1

To my father and mother,
who modeled justice and mercy
in loving correction

Contents

Introduction

A Parent's Longing

I was observing a scene that blocked the aisle in a busy grocery store. A mother with three small boys was showing a mixture of embarrassment, frustration, and hopelessness. Two of her boys were running here and there, then rushing to her side with loud demands that she buy this item or that. Each boy was out-whining and out-howling the other, their voices no doubt heard throughout the store.

"You're wasting time!" she told them in an exasperated tone. The boys' demands grew only louder.

I ached with empathy for this harried mother. We've all had similar grocery store experiences of our own. And they're painful. We long for our children to behave well, and for good reasons—we want them to understand and value the right things and to live in the freedom that comes with self-control.

So often, our hope for all that seems battered or even crushed.

My heart goes out to the downhearted and flustered mothers of young children who know things have gotten out of hand. I've spoken and prayed with scores of them. I feel for the mother in South Dakota who asked me how to change the tone in their home. I admire the mother in Wisconsin who invited me to help her and her husband in promoting sweet and godly interactions in their family.

I've known what it's like to earnestly desire help with parenting, and wanting keenly not to squander the early years in our children's lives. I've prayed for readers of this book, that God would use these pages to help you, not shame you.

The aim of this book is to throw you a rope, not an anchor. Think of this book as an arm around your shoulder, a gentle pat on the back, and a nod that says, "You can do this. I'm pulling for you. God will help you. Your children will thank you later."

Parenting is sometimes painful, but it can also be joyful. I think of these words of John in Scripture: "I have no greater joy than to hear that my children are walking in the truth" (3 John 4). For parents, there's no greater joy than children walking in truth, yet many parents can identify with the opposite: there's no greater misery than knowing their children's behavior is outside the truth, a departure from what's best for them. How can we correct our children and get them back on the rails of truth and goodness?

Often, correction is done poorly. Our well-intended attempts can be too harsh or too lenient or too complicated. But correction *can* be done well. How can we correct our children without becoming harsh drill sergeants?

The apostles corrected the churches, shepherds correct straying sheep, good teachers correct student errors—and loving parents confront wrongdoing in their children. But how is this done *well*?

My aim in these pages is to help you better understand good correction.

Part 1

WHAT'S AT STAKE?

1

Why the Struggle?

Parents can be confused or even clueless when it comes to correcting their children effectively. Often they have wrong assumptions about it. Wrong assumptions have tripped me up as a parent—and they might be tripping you up as well. These wrong assumptions can center on issues as basic as why our children disobey and why we ought to correct them.

What *is* correction, anyway? Here's a two-part definition that I think is helpful.

Corrective discipline means:

(1) Identifying actions or attitudes of your child that are unacceptable when weighed against clear and explicit standards, then
(2) acting promptly and decisively to move your child in the direction of compliance with those standards.

Later, we'll inspect each phrase of that definition more closely. I pray this definition will help you, and that it fits with your own good intentions as a parent. Why do we struggle with making our good intentions happen? The reasons for our struggle grow clearer when we look deeper at why children disobey and why we as parents can be slow to correct them.

Why Do Children Disobey?

Our children can sometimes astonish us with how quickly and repeatedly they disobey. Shouldn't they just naturally know better? We look at them and think, *What's the matter with you?*

Well . . . sin, of course, is the matter with all of us. Including children. Even the most adorable little tyke is a natural-born sinner.

Sometimes we speak our frustration out loud: "What's *wrong* with you?" But parents shouldn't request that kind of explanation for misbehavior (especially since such indicting speech can instill irrational guilt in a son or daughter, like that experienced by children who are abused). What parents should be after is the child's compliance with clearly understood standards.

Besides your child's sin nature, maybe there's nothing "wrong" with him. The problem may be that he has been repeatedly rewarded for behaving the way he does. He's simply functioning according to the way God designed rewards and reinforcement to operate. (We'll talk more about this later.)

Children are not naturally obedient. The problem lies in the opposite direction. The little fellows are sinners—and sin hardens. The Bible talks about our daily potential of being "hardened by the deceitfulness of sin" (Heb. 3:13). We're told in that verse to therefore "exhort one another every day, as long as it is called 'today.'" That's true for our children, too; they require corrective exhortations.

Obedience must be learned. The good news is that it can be! Weary and beleaguered parents can take hope in knowing this: children *can* be taught to respectfully obey. Children require some assembly—plus clear instruction and guidelines, and the kind of training that demonstrates your genuine love.

We're All After Happiness

Like you and me, children are naturally prone to pursue their own happiness without regard to what pleases God or anybody else. In their native sinfulness, they stubbornly disobey out of a desire to pursue pleasure in a way that isn't constrained by any outside authority.

In his *Pensées*, Blaise Pascal famously gave the world this reminder: "All men seek happiness. This is without exception. Whatever different means they employ, they all tend to this end."[1] Children are no exception. They're seeking happiness, and again and again they figure that disobedience will gain them more happiness than obedience will.

After all, what do we suppose makes *us* happy? We think we know, don't we? Children believe the same about themselves. And they're pursuing it. They esteem their own plan above all others, no matter how foolish that plan might be. I can speak from my own personal experience as a child: we're born naturally foolish and in need of correction, just as the Bible tells us. "Folly is bound up in the heart of a child, but the rod of discipline drives it far from him" (Prov. 22:15).

The fall—humanity's plunge into sin—threw all of nature into the need for correction. The culminating event of earthly history is when Jesus returns to make his grand correction, making all things new. But that hasn't happened yet. Meanwhile,

---

1. Blaise Pascal, *Pensées*, Harvard Classics ed., trans. William Finlayson Trotter (New York: F. F. Collier & Son, 1910), 7.425.

our children need correction. As we all do. We need correction because we affirm wrong things, or we affirm good things over against better things, or we affirm good things from wrong motives. That's our bent.

When we honestly face up to this sinfulness in our children, do we then give up any expectation that they'll obey us? No. But we shouldn't be surprised when they don't obey us the first time, every time.

And when they don't, we correct—or we should.

Does this require that I watch my kids like a hawk, looking over their shoulder all day long? No. Good parents enjoy empowering their children to try new adventures, expanding each child's understanding of the pleasures to be found in God's world. But parental permissiveness should never make allowance for defiant disobedience.

Why Do Parents Hold Back?

If correction simply means we identify unacceptable actions or attitudes in our child, and then act promptly and decisively to move that child in the right direction of compliance, why do we so often hesitate?

Sometimes, it's because firm correction makes us feel guilty. No good parent wants to come across as a dictator.

At other times, it's because we don't see the value in corrective discipline. It seems to make little difference, so why bother?

At other times, we don't want to upset the child.

And sometimes, we're just plain weary.

I'm no stranger to any of those feelings. But a number of wrong assumptions may be lurking behind them. When our children are unruly and disobedient—when the moment's ripe for correction—all kinds of fears and worries and doubts can cause parents to hold back.

Like these:

> My child will think I've lost my affection for him or her.
> My child will stop loving and respecting me.
> I run the risk of damaging my child's self-esteem.
> I'll stifle my child's personality, creativity, and drive to explore.
> I'll cause my child to be afraid of me.

If you've had those thoughts, it's helpful to remember certain truths. For example, when a child is rebelling, the child in that moment is far less interested in your affection than in getting his or her own way. You might mistakenly assume that your affection and patience alone will miraculously remedy your child's misbehavior. Yes, when pigs fly, oceans run dry, and December's in July. Your child may not take kindly to you in the moment you apply corrective discipline, but a child's love is swiftly rekindled—and deepened and solidified in the process of receiving wise correction.

Or let's think about the danger of damaging a child's self-esteem. I'm a strong proponent of building up a child's self-*acceptance*. But that's not the same as self-*esteem*. Self-acceptance is necessary and good, but self-*esteem* plagues the world. Prisons are full of people who esteem no one but self.

Children (like adults) are naturally self-centered. No baby in the nursery is crying because some *other* baby is wet or hungry. Infants come out of the womb entirely self-preoccupied and quite content to let the entire universe cater to them. Their self-will is fully formed. They are us.

When we worry that our child will perceive our corrective discipline as unloving, we forget God's higher wisdom about genuine love. He tells us, "Whoever spares the rod hates his son, but he who loves him is diligent to discipline him" (Prov. 13:24). When we refrain from correction, do we subconsciously think we're wiser than God?

True love means that parents will give their children objective "outside" feedback on the true condition of their sinful little hearts: "The heart is deceitful above all things, and desperately sick; who can understand it?" (Jer. 17:9). Correction exists because errors and omissions exist, and because sin exists. Corrections are undertaken because of love. Love implements correction in order to protect the loved one from heaping up negative consequences, to his or her regret.

God knows that discipline and obedience are required before a child's God-given abilities can truly flourish. It's a misunderstanding to think that practicing firm, decisive, consistent discipline will interfere in any way with your children's proper development. Christlikeness does not develop accidentally.

The Fear Factor

I admit there's a fine line—and perhaps a tricky distinction—between destructively fearing a parent and having a healthy regard for that parent's authority to reward and punish. This dynamic mirrors our relationship with God, where genuine fear is warranted. God is not to be trifled with: "Fear God and keep his commandments, for this is the whole duty of man" (Eccles. 12:13). Moses once asked the Lord, "Who understands the power of Your anger? Your wrath matches the fear that is due you" (Ps. 90:11 HCSB).

Where can we flee to escape God's just wrath? We flee to God himself, to his mercy. We pray with the psalmist, "Be to me a rock of refuge, to which I may continually come; you have given the command to save me, for you are my rock and my fortress" (Ps. 71:3).

We fear God because he loves us so much that he threatens to do terrible things if we run from him. As C. S. Lewis famously taught us through Aslan in The Chronicles of Narnia, God certainly isn't safe—but he's *good*. In a healthy parent-child relationship, the child will possess a general apprehension regarding the consequences of defying his parent. Growing up, I knew that if I sassed my mother, I'd be in a heap of trouble with my father. But I also knew that if I spoke respectfully to Mom, there was nothing to fear from Dad in that regard. The child who discovers that his parents punish only when he does wrong will be more apt to avoid wrongdoing. There's punishment to dread—but only if you deserve it.

I take it for granted that good parents desire to show kindness and compassion toward their children. God himself has established the template: "As a father shows compassion to his children, so the LORD shows compassion *to those who fear him*" (Ps. 103:13). With tender care, wise parents teach children to have the *right* fear—to fear what warrants fear—but not to be anxious, jittery, skittish, or timid. We're not aiming to make cowards of our children, but bold and heroic champions. Correction aims to shape them, not harm them.

If our children fear us without delighting in us, they'll find no rest in our company. If our children delight in us without the right fear, we'll become their vending machine, and when the machine doesn't dispense what they want, they just may utter curses and inflict hostility toward us.

Note also that an authoritative approach that may *invoke* fear is not the same as an approach that is fear-*based*. There are things one might naturally fear (crossing the street at the wrong moment), but that fear is not injurious—in fact, it prevents injury. Such fear is healthy, not paralyzing or psychopathic.

Love and fear are not necessarily at odds or mutually exclusive. God loves his own, and he commands them to fear him. In his relationship with us, God doesn't restrict himself to doing only what provokes our positive feelings. Sometimes he causes our momentary pain—which is meant to be transforming and corrective, driving us away from destructive attitudes and behaviors. He doesn't cease to be good when he disciplines us. All along he's aiming at "the peaceful fruit of righteousness." Pain isn't his purpose, but his means: "For the Lord disciplines the one he loves, and chastises every son whom he receives. . . . For the moment all discipline seems painful rather than pleasant, but later it yields the peaceful fruit of righteousness to those who have been trained by it" (Heb. 12:6, 11).

I join the myriad of individuals who, upon receiving parental correction, did not find it enjoyable at the time. But now, years later, I'm extremely grateful for it. It's a mistake to think you should never do anything that your child finds painful. *No* discipline is pleasant at the time. Wise, corrective discipline always has an element of pain and discomfort. But God promises a fruitful result. It will eventually usher in peace—even if, for the time being, conflict escalates.

Behavior Change versus Heart Change

If our correction promotes a child's *external* conformity to our instructions (and to God's) but leaves the heart unchanged—won't that merely suck our child into outward conformity, moralism, and legalism, and away from heart transformation and sincere cooperation? While children are still spiritually unregenerate, maybe it's useless or counterproductive for parents to correct them when they fail to obey the commands they're given (tell the truth, obey your parents, don't steal your brother's things, put on your pajamas, don't throw your applesauce). How could such a child's obedience be genuine?

It is unwise to pit behavioral change against heart change as though it's either/or—because it's *both/and*. Wise discipline looks beyond simply altering the child's behavior; it aims toward impressing the heart. But on the way to the heart, good discipline *does* shape behavior. Wise discipline doesn't skip over behavioral change, even while praying for the child's heart change.

Wisdom doesn't settle for changed behaviors, but presses on toward the goal of attitudinal change that only God fully creates and sustains. But the path to such heart change is often *through* the measured pain of discipline—the awakening rod of correction, the consequential misery of reaping what one's mischief has sown.

Discipline aims at fostering a specified pattern of character, in the strength God supplies.

We want to address the heart, not just outward behaviors. Meanwhile, we also want to address those problematic outward behaviors before they introduce undesirable consequences. Proverbs 20:11 tells us, "Even a child makes himself known by his acts, by whether his conduct is pure and upright." The child's true character becomes *known* by his actions—which means behavior! But corrective discipline that addresses behavior is not mere behavior*ism*.

Moreover, even outward yet unredeemed conformity to godly ways is ultimately better *for the child* than nonconformity and defiance. It's also better for all those who have to share the room and the community (and the grocery store aisles) with that child. When parents restrain the egocentric bent of defiant children, we help shape their little consciences (even before they're born again) while also making it easier for these children to later get along in society.

More importantly, requiring obedience from children can awaken awareness of their own sin nature and their need for Christ to be their substitute. It can show them their further need for inner transformation. A child will have difficulty grasping the meaning of the cross if parents haven't required him to confront his own sinful impulses as wrongful.

Paul tells us (in Gal. 3:24) that the law with its rules and regulations is a schoolmaster to bring us to Christ, but that result is less likely in a child's life if biblical standards of behavior are not taken seriously by the adults around the child. It's right and necessary for parents to require children to do some things their little sinful natures dislike. Requiring a child to do something when he would rather do something else is an excellent and necessary way not only to shape behavior, but also to awaken the child to his attitudes.

It's foolish and irresponsible for parents to think they can do little or nothing while waiting for their children to "see the light," experience regeneration, and turn over a new leaf. To not correct disobedience is to entrench it.

Further, a child's simple good behavior and civility (not biting your neighbor, saying please and thank you, speaking in a respectful tone of voice) can come from the heart later, even if for now it comes "only" from parental enforcement.

So we aim for outward conformity, but not outward conformity *only*. We also aim for inward transformation, knowing that when inner heart transformation happens, it will be followed by outward cooperation. Heart change in our child is our desire in corrective discipline, and we know that what's necessary for heart change is God. Meanwhile, behavioral methods—especially rewards and punishments—can be a means to capturing the child's attention for introduction of the gospel. Wise correction can get the attention of the head so that instruction can make its way to the heart.

We can't force our children (or anyone else) to supremely value the supremely valuable, for we cannot make them actually see it as valuable. But we can display it as being superior, and we can discipline our children to look, even if they don't look seeingly just yet.

Genuine obedience to God's standards must spring from the heart, and we can't coerce a child to worship and obey God with genuine heartfelt earnestness. Rebellion also flows from the heart. While we can't change the rebellion, we can attach firm and clear associations to rebellious actions so that in the child's understanding, pain becomes associated with naughtiness. Our son or daughter begins to discover that refusal to live in accord with God's ways results eventually in disaster and regret. For a sinner, the thrill of misbehavior can seem to be its own "reward"; we as parents are being neither kind nor wise if we let that impression continue, giving a child the false impression that life brings no painful consequences for misbehavior.

When correction is done well, it does *not* derail heart change, which is absolutely essential, but honors God, who is the foundation and pinnacle of what is right. We want our children to honor God, and requiring children to honor parents honors the God who commands children to do exactly that.

We cannot change our children's hearts, but if they go through life never having to complete an unpleasant assignment or yield to the leadership of an authority, we're foolish to think we've prepared them to yield to God.

2

When We Fail to
Correct Our Children

When I was at the tire store, a little girl (perhaps three years old) was not only failing to follow her mother's directions but doing the opposite of what she was told to do. When the mother said, "Come here," the child ran off in the other direction, giggling.

The mother glanced at me and the clerk with an awkward grin and a shrug. An observer could read a lot into her expression. She might well have been saying, "I'm sorry, my child doesn't seem to want to cooperate today. Perhaps it's a phase. I hope you can bear with me until she outgrows it." And off the mother went to chase down her cute little girl.

Cute, yes. But also harmful.

Soon the computer system at the store went down. The clerks couldn't wait on customers, since work orders and billing and credit transactions were online. Then one mechanic after another became stymied in their car stalls, since diagnostic computers were locked up.

The local manager telephoned the company headquarters in another city to troubleshoot the computer system and follow steps to get it back up and running. The store's entire business was down for about a half hour. Meanwhile I and other customers waited in the checkout line to retrieve our vehicles.

The truth emerged that the cute little disobedient girl had gone behind the counter and pushed a pretty colored button on one of the computing towers.

In this unfortunate episode we could point to several contributing factors (such as computers within a child's reach). But the point here is that the trouble wouldn't have happened if the harried mother had promptly corrected her little girl's antics.

Obedience matters. Disobedience brings unintended consequences.

Consider the costs of not correcting our children. What happens when we fail to act promptly and decisively to move our child toward compliance with the acceptable standards we've identified and made explicit? Those consequences are larger than we probably expect.

Harm to Our Role as Parents

Our authority, our credibility, and even our trustworthiness as parents are at stake. To give direction or commands to our children and then not enforce them is to teach them that our instruction means nothing. The character development of both parent and child is at stake in the issue of whether we follow through on our instructions and commands. It's by observing their parents that children learn to speak with integrity, to mean what they say, and to follow through on their word.

Failure to practice correction can lead the child to distrust you. If our no doesn't mean no, then the word is not only pointless—it's a lie. Such falsehood, even if unintended, can destroy the child's confidence in the trustworthiness of the parent's word. For example, if you tell your young child, "Don't touch that," but do nothing when she proceeds to touch it, your instruction has come to mean nothing, and your daughter's trust in your words is diminished.

If you accept unacceptable behavior—defiance, needless delay in obedience, indifference—why shouldn't your child conclude that what you *claim* to be important really isn't, after all? The author of Hebrews mentions how "we have had earthly fathers who disciplined us and we respected them" (12:9). But if your children aren't consistently and lovingly corrected for their infractions, they'll tend to disrespect you as a weak parent who issues empty commands not worthy of respect.

Failure to enforce your instructions teaches disregard for your instructions—and ultimately for God's instructions. After all, obedience to parents isn't a concept invented by parents, but by God.

Eroding All Our Efforts

Of course, correcting misbehaving children isn't the only thing good parents do, or even the main thing. More importantly, good parents commend what's commendable in their children. They enjoy their children, affirm God's gifts to them, serve them, and drench the household in the ways of the Lord (as we see in Deut. 6:6–9).

But parental failure to correct can torpedo all those other parental efforts. Everything from music lessons to academics to household chores to forging healthy friendships can be held hostage by not first establishing that the parent will follow through on what he or she commands. Furthermore, peace in the home will be left hanging in the balance.

A child's self-control, which ought to be fostered by proper parental correction, can also become a casualty. Children have natural God-given abilities just waiting to be developed and refined. But our sons and daughters probably won't excel in developing those abilities without developing self-restraint along the way. Even the "natural" athlete becomes a champion only by enduring rigorous exercise, drills, training, coaching, repetition, and self-denial. If he's unwilling to undergo those rigors, he won't enjoy the triumph of significant victory. The path to achieving such victory starts early, with corrective discipline from parents.

Also, if your children aren't required to obey, they'll miss out on the enjoyment of being commended for obedience. If children are allowed to disregard parental instruction, they flounder on the way to discovering—if they ever do—whether they might be recognized for doing something truly good. Meanwhile, they'll begin to wonder if you truly care.

A Downward Spiral

An undisciplined toddler will not grow out of his naughtiness by himself. Accommodation to a child's tantrums will lead to more tantrums and then more accommodation, in an endless cycle.

Give in to your child's demands, and you'll develop a demanding child. Uncorrected rudeness, insolence, and sassiness can harden over time into worldly decadence, a pattern that becomes even harder to correct when the child is older. It's less likely that a child will "grow out of it" than that he'll grow into larger and more harmful expressions of his inner rebelliousness.

His challenges to his parents will grow in scale as he gets older—breaking curfews, skipping church, skipping school, choosing corrupting friends, using vehicles irresponsibly, experimenting with harmful substances, falling into sexual immorality, and more. The training of a child sets the table for his adult years. "Train up a child in the way he should go; even when he is old he will not depart from it" (Prov. 22:6).

Increasing Danger

One winter, two teenagers disregarded warnings about thin ice on Lake Minnetonka, drove their car out on the ice, and broke through. One drowned in the frigid waters, and the other froze to death on the ice. It can be very costly to ignore warnings.

A child's uncorrected defiance and disobedience are danger signals for the parent, warning of the worst possible outcomes when correction isn't applied. Children who presume there's no law higher than their own desires will become further ensnared by fleshly appetites. Paul calls it slavery (Rom. 6:16; Titus 3:3). Absence of correction tends to solidify the child's impression that he is king and you, the parent, are his subject. Allowing disobedience to your commands teaches the child that he's the highest authority. Not reinforcing boundaries conveys that we really don't care whether our child does good or evil.

If *you* don't harness your children, someone else will. Your children are in a war, and undisciplined children are more vulnerable to being devoured by enemies within and without.

Romans 1 teaches that all human beings are born truth suppressors. One of the truths we keep trying to suppress is that we don't—and can't—justify ourselves before God. The meaning of our existence and the establishment of what's truly best for our well-being are not things we invent; they're established by our Creator, ready to be discovered by us. Our purpose, our righteousness, our well-being, and our joy are all rooted not in us, but in another—our God. It's good for children to learn this early.

Children whose stubborn self-will isn't consistently confronted will fail to live humbly under the Romans 1 reality that they're truth-suppressing self-justifiers. Their consequence-producing stubbornness will become more and more entrenched. Children left to themselves are prone to follow their own indifference to God. Later, it's difficult to disabuse spoiled adolescents of a narcissistic bent that went unchecked in childhood. Wise tolerance has limits. When we tolerate defiance, we plant seeds for a profoundly regrettable future.

Jonathan Edwards gave the illustration of how a small sapling is easier to pull up than a tree that "has sent forth its roots deep into the earth," then drew this parallel: "If children continue to spend their time in sin, then God may abandon them to their own hardness of heart, making their chances of conversion later in life very slim."[1]

Martin Luther emphasized the same danger:

> The first destroyers of their own children are those who neglect them and knowingly permit them to grow up without the training and admonition of the Lord. Even if they do not harm them by a bad example, they still destroy them by yielding to them (*permissione*). They love them too much according to the flesh and pamper them, saying: They are children, they do not understand what they are doing. And they are speaking the truth. But neither does a dog or a horse or a mule understand what it is doing. However, see how they learn to go, to come, to obey, to do and leave undone what they do not understand. . . . These parents will, therefore, bear the sins of their children because they make these sins their own.[2]

---

1. Jonathan Edwards, "The Time of Youth Is the Best Time to Be Improved for Religious Purposes," in *To the Rising Generation*, ed. Don Kistler (Lake Mary, FL: Soli Deo Gloria, 2005), 18.

2. Martin Luther, *What Luther Says: An Anthology*, compiled by Ewald M. Plass, 3 vols. (Saint Louis: Concordia, 1959), 1:139.

Luther also wrote this: "Parents can perform no more damaging bit of work than to neglect their offspring, to let them curse, swear, learn indecent words and songs, and permit them to live as they please."[3]

And this: "A father can perform no act that is more unfatherly than sparing the rod and allowing the little child to have its own wanton way."[4]

The dangers of failing to correctively discipline our children are as dreadfully real as they can possibly be. Wise Solomon expressed it this way: "Discipline your son, for there is hope; do not set your heart on putting him to death" (Prov. 19:18). I think Solomon had in mind that there will come a time in each child's life when correcting him will be practically impossible, and if we don't correct our children well before that time, it's the same as setting our heart on their destruction. We're setting them up to self-destruct.

It's too late to head for the storm shelter when the tornado is overhead, or to lock the gate after the cattle are out, or to be careful once the milk is already spilt. But, as Solomon says, right now "there is hope." That's what the next chapter will point us to.

---

3. Luther, *What Luther Says*, 1:141
4. Luther, *What Luther Says*, 1:139.

3

When We Faithfully
Correct Our Children

It costs a lot to correctively discipline our children. It requires time, forethought, interruptions, prayer, reading books like this, and the continuing hard work of actual confronting.

Because it's so costly, we need motivation in order to do it. There must be a payoff, a sufficient reward to make us willing to tackle the endeavor. Otherwise it's too daunting. Why bother?

Let's consider the benefits and blessings of properly correcting our children. The wise, corrective discipline of our children glorifies the truth-speaking God of the Bible, honors parents (*all* parents, as well as the specific child's parents), protects our children, strengthens the church, serves society, and gives hope to the nations.

The Rewards of Faithful Correction

As a demonstration of our genuine love, faithful parental discipline assures our children of *belongingness*. This is one of the supreme benefits and blessings of discipline, and it's crucial to every child's identity. It's a belongingness that points to the fatherhood of God, as this profound passage indicates: "It is for discipline that you have to endure. *God is treating you as sons.* For what son is there whom his father does not discipline? If you are left without discipline, in which all have participated, then *you are illegitimate children and not sons*" (Heb. 12:7–8). (Emphasizing belongingness as a demonstration of the fatherhood of God in your loving discipline is important for adopted children.)

Far more than simply molding their behavior, our corrective discipline makes our children wiser as they better grasp God's fatherly love, guidance, and purposes for their lives. Even before a child experiences a transformed heart through Christian conversion, disciplinary correction awakens him to the stark reality that he's not the only person in the universe, and his will is not the only will. There's a thing called *others*.

As our children are disciplined, they learn that the universe is designed with cause-and-effect relationships pointing to a Designer. Children start to discover this when their own violations of parental instructions are followed swiftly and consistently with correction. This cause-and-effect relationship is a pillar of their own self-discipline (which is what we're aiming for). Actions have consequences. Your child may be a sinner, but he should learn early that he cannot sin with impunity.

Parental discipline, writes pastor and missionary Wilbur Bruinsma, "is a necessity in the life of a child because it teaches him what sin is, and that sin will be punished. The child is trained by discipline to understand that God holds man accountable for sin and God will punish it in His justice."[1]

---

1. Wilbur Bruinsma, "Martin Luther: Training Children in the Home" in *The Standard Bearer*, 78/2002, no. 2 (October 15, 2001), https://standardbearer.rfpa.org/index.php?q=node/46091.

The pain of correction can awaken a naughty child to the reality of his naughtiness—no excuses, no buffering. Even before heart transformation occurs, effective parental correction can help a child learn to recognize a standard, so that later, after conversion, he'll marvel that he now wants to behave righteously (thus honoring his parents).

No child can be "disciplined" into Christian faith. We're all saved by grace, not discipline. But discipline can subdue defiance that prevents the child from sitting still long enough to hear the gospel. Listening to the words of the gospel isn't sufficient on its own to produce faith, but faith won't spring up in the absence of hearing. So we teach our children to listen. Waffling on our commands teaches children to *not* listen.

Teaching immediate compliance builds children who are not only wiser but also safer. In the backyard where his son was playing, a father shouted, "Drop to your hands and knees and crawl to me right now!" While this may at first seem harsh, the dad could see what the son could not: a poisonous snake slowly lowering himself from a tree branch just above the boy.

Prompt obedience to proper correction builds trust in you and your word. Obedience first, discussion about snakes later.

Our Children Become a Blessing to Others

Corrective discipline—which leads to a child's self-discipline—opens the door to more freedom and more accomplishment for that child. It helps children to achieve what can be gained only through inner desire, self-restraint, and personal behavior governed by voluntary, self-willed commitment.

The Olympic athlete voluntarily exercises his body strenuously without anyone threatening him with punishment. The musician keeps practicing and practicing, not because someone is standing over him with a stick, but because he has an inner desire to let that piece of music lift the spirit through his trained fingers. One of my heroes practiced the cello until his fingers bled; no one forced him to do this.

The child's self-discipline is therefore a significant goal of the parent's enforced discipline. Along the way, our children will grow in getting along better with the rest of society. After all, people respond more readily to a cooperative child than they do to a Tasmanian devil who won't take direction. That fact should be a reminder that we discipline a mouthy and defiant child not because we've had our personal sensitivities offended, but because it's not good *for the child's sake* to go on being that way.

Throughout childhood, children become increasingly fixed in their attitude toward authority—all authority. Consistent, loving, firm parental correction in the early years will pave the way for the child to have good working relationships later with teachers, coaches, employers, government officials, store clerks, and anyone else having a position of legitimate authority.

In training a child, we aren't merely shaping a particular behavior in a particular moment. We're shaping lifelong habits that help the child build a good name—even before he becomes a believer. Solomon tells us that a well-disciplined child "will give delight to your heart" (Prov. 29:17). Cooperative children, trained to be that way by their parents, will also become a delight to others.

Good for Them, Good for Us

Committing yourself to doing a good job in disciplining your child will encourage you to reflect carefully on what's truly important. And that's a good thing for any parent.

There's a sense in which raising our children raises us. When I was young, I thought the sequence went something like this: *Grow up . . . get married . . . have children.* But now I think it's more like this: *Grow . . . get married . . . grow up* (because marriage requires it) *. . . have children . . . grow up some more* (because being a good parent requires it).

I've often said to my grown children, "You raised me." The presence of children in our lives exposes our character flaws, providing us with humbling opportunities for change.

We're not only training youngsters for the future; we're also training ourselves for today and for whatever future eventually arrives. Disciplining our children is good for us parents.

Wisely practiced, our parental correction will help clear our conscience. We'll know we haven't shirked our responsibility under God. What's more, when parents alertly and consistently discipline their child's *attitudes* at an early age, the disciplining of *behaviors* will become more rare. Enforcement will become less and less necessary. It gets easier, even if it's strenuous at the beginning. But ease is not the chief goal. Our goal is for God to get glory because our children enjoy him.

Be Willing to Invest

Settle it in your mind: effective, God-pleasing child-rearing will require your diligence and endurance.

It's certain that we as parents will make mistakes in our practice of discipline. We nevertheless have a responsibility under God to persevere in doing our children good: "And let us not grow weary of doing good, for in due season we will reap, if we do not give up. So then, as we have opportunity, let us do good to everyone, and especially to those who are of the household of faith" (Gal. 6:9–10).

In the process of raising our children, God will permit us to become weary, which then exposes our true convictions—what we're committed to doing when it's not easy, when we're exhausted. God provides an enabling grace tailored for just such a moment, customized for each individual parent. (This book is intended to be a little part of that grace.)

God supernaturally aids conviction that is tested when the going becomes very difficult. Parents in such moments are being tested in the same way that a manufacturer will test a brand of epoxy to see if it will hold. Adversity tests parents to see if their love for God and their children will hold genuine. And genuine love never gives up (1 Cor. 13:7–8).

Your resolute commitment to consistency and follow-through will be aided by the principle of preemption. How important something is to us will be demonstrated and confirmed by what we permit it to interrupt. For example, we know that tornado warnings on television are important not by the nice clothes of the announcer or the animated graphics on the map or the high-definition color broadcasting. We know the warnings are considered important because of what they interrupt: namely, everything else.

What preempts what? We let things of lesser importance be interrupted by more important things.

Your children will know that your directives are important when you interrupt everything else in order to enforce them. If you're going to show that your word is important, you must interrupt what you're doing to enforce your word, to correct your child, and show that your words have value. Put down your phone, turn away from what you were doing, and discipline your child. Pull off the road and settle the matter.

For parents to make correction the priority it needs to be, they must be willing to drop what they're doing and *act*. Let the child know in advance that if and when the moment comes, you fully intend to drop what you're doing and correct him. This cannot be a bluff. It must be demonstrated by *action*, not mere words. It takes consistency backed by willing resolve.

All this requires a heavy investment on the part of parents—a commitment of attentiveness, energy, and lots more. But the investment brings sweet dividends.

You Are the Solution

Although children are sinners by nature, when they misbehave, the solution almost always lies with the parent. *Your* behavior is generally the key to your child's behavior problems. (There are exceptions, but they're . . . well, exceptions. They are rare.)

Think how often this happens: children who don't whine to adult caregivers (such as nursery attendants, preschool workers, schoolteachers, babysitters) will immediately start whining when their parent walks in. What's the variable? *The parent.* The point in saying this is not to beat up parents, but to offer hope and encouragement. By changing what *you* as the parent do, you can change what your children do.

There *is* great hope.

And there *is* help.

Part 2

ESSENTIALS OF CORRECTIVE DISCIPLINE

4

Clarifying Our Aim

Let's look again at our working definition for what this book is all about. It starts this way:

> Corrective discipline means identifying actions or attitudes of your child that are unacceptable . . .

Notice the focus on *your* child. When considering correction, context and jurisdiction always matter. Parents have a divinely appointed jurisdiction over *their* children that others simply don't possess. It's a responsibility parents bear before God. They set the curfew or dress code or whatever for their own household, but it's not in their purview to make such policy for the homes of others.

In your home, you as parent are accountable to God for the establishment and enforcement of the house rules you decide on. While your children are living under your roof and eating your groceries, you have the right and the responsibility to set standards for their behavior and to enforce them.

The attitudes and actions that qualify as "unacceptable"—the specific behaviors to be corrected—will thus vary from household to household. In principle, however, this is what every parent should particularly and consistently correct: *defiant disobedience*.

Changing Your Child's Trajectory

Here's our full definition again.

Corrective discipline means:

(1) Identifying actions or attitudes of your child that are unacceptable when weighed against clear and explicit standards—then

(2) acting promptly and decisively to move your child in the direction of compliance with those standards.

Correction doesn't merely make suggestions or even give orders. It *moves* the child. If the child's trajectory isn't redirected, correction hasn't taken place. In a nutshell, correction is basically:

No, *not* that.

Yes, *this*.

Yes, *now*.

Meanwhile, when we correct our children, our higher purpose is to help recalibrate their compasses and turn their heads and eyes toward True North—with the prayer that they'll learn to see God and delight in him with all their hearts.

While we can't prepare a child directly for every specific situation they'll encounter in their lives, we can prepare them *generally* for every situation. Our aim is their Christlikeness:

Him we proclaim, warning everyone and teaching everyone with all wisdom, that we may present everyone *mature in Christ*. (Col. 1:28)

For those whom [God] foreknew he also predestined to be *conformed to the image of his Son*. (Rom. 8:29)

Such Christlikeness helps accomplish the highest and ultimate objective of our corrective discipline, which is to glorify God.

The goal for our children is not independence, but responsibility. We're not aiming to make independent adults. There *are* no independent adults. All adults are dependent on God and his means of grace, including each other as such means. But all of us are responsible. We're aiming to develop children into *responsible* adults. We want our children to grow to handle their responsibilities responsibly.

Our aim is to raise children who are positioned well to exalt Jesus, the glorious and final Corrector who needed no correction (though many tried to force it upon him). When I speak of Jesus as the glorious and final Corrector, I mean that in the end he'll be the final judge of right and wrong, the granter of rewards and punishments, and the separator of wheat from chaff, sheep from goats, and true believers from those whom he "never knew" (Matt. 7:23).

We cannot produce belief in our children, but we can teach them to stand still long enough to hear the gospel of this Jesus in whom we pray they'll believe.

A Part of Something Bigger

Imagine a spacious, sprawling castle of countless rooms. The job of parenting is like that—it's vast and complex, with many areas, many concerns.

Corrective discipline is like one room inside that huge structure. Correction isn't the whole castle of parenting, but it's a valuable part.

To refine and strengthen that picture even more, think of that structure as a great castle of love and care. There ought to be no division between parents who lovingly care about their children and parents who rightly care about corrective discipline. They should be one and the same.

Caring deeply about your child isn't the same as loving him well by disciplining him, but each thing requires the other. *Effective* care includes discipline.

Firm consistency in our discipline is not mean or harmful or unloving. What *is* mean and harmful and unloving (though unintentionally) is failing to expect your child's compliance, and failing to actively, consistently pursue it. Such failure invites your child to a regrettable future.

Wise correction is regret management—for all concerned.

Discipline doesn't destroy the child—but attacks the things that *would* destroy him. To exercise discipline of your child is to be kind as well as empowering, preparing your child to exercise his expanding powers more fully in the freedom that comes from self-control. We accomplish that best and easiest by remembering three core imperatives for wise correction:

1. Keep it God-centered.
2. Speak truth—always mean what you say.
3. Reward obedience, not disobedience.

We'll study these core essentials in the following three chapters.

5

Keep It God-Centered

Let's recall again our guiding definition for correction:

Corrective discipline means:

(1) Identifying actions or attitudes of your child that are unacceptable when weighed against clear and explicit standards—then
(2) acting promptly and decisively to move your child in the direction of compliance with those standards.

You might ask: Where's God in that definition?

Well, he's not explicitly mentioned. But he's implicit in the actions the definition points to: *identifying, weighing, taking decisive action,* and *moving.*

Being God-Dependent

First, as parents we're utterly dependent on God's help in *identifying* what we need to correct in our children. Otherwise we remain blind or indifferent.

Second, we're largely adrift without God's biblical standards when it comes to *weighing* what's rightly acceptable and unacceptable in our children's behavior and attitudes. We need a fixed moral center.

Third, we need the Spirit's enablement to *take decisive action* in a timely fashion. Otherwise we might remain passive or fearful or overly hesitant.

Finally, our children will not *move* in the direction of compliance unless the Spirit works in them; it's God who's at work in them both to will and to do his good pleasure (Phil. 2:13).

Is it all up to God then? Yes and no. Our infinitely wise and perfect God is determinative, yes—but imperfect parents are the instruments in the Redeemer's hand.

And his hand is busy! My own parenting has improved as I've increasingly embraced the assumption that the Lord is sovereignly at work in people, including the sinful hearts of young children. And he brings about his ends through means.

God's role is central and essential. Therefore, we embrace dependence upon his Holy Spirit. Heart change is a divine work. This book's core message is that corrective discipline in its fullest scope is a divine work. It's not mainly about you or by you, but him.

We noted earlier that we cannot directly change the hearts of our children, but parental discipline can plow up the soil for good seed. The heart of your child is the heart of the matter. In our discipline, we're wise to continually ask, "Are we getting to the heart of the matter?"

In commenting on the purpose of such discipline aimed at the heart, Matt Chandler puts it this way: "It is to gather all the kindling we can around them in the hopes that the Holy Spirit would ignite it."[1]

---

1. Matt Chandler, "Parenting: An Awareness of Our Need" (sermon on Colossians 3:20–21, The Village Church, Flower Mound, TX, July 18, 2010), at, http://www.tvc resources.net/resource-library/sermons/parenting-an-awareness-of-our-need/.

Because God's role is essential in all this, we pray. We read his revealed instructions. And we apply the means he has appointed.

In the life of the child, parents play the key human role as God's agent. Parents are stewards of their children, not owners. The child's responsibility is to obey, and the parent's responsibility is to teach obedience, reward it, and correct disobedience.

In our God-given parenting role, depending on his help so often means depending on the help of other people. That's true in other areas of your life, and it's true in disciplining your children. So don't work alone. Get more adults involved. "Gramma said to put your jacket on before you go out," says the dad as he backs up Gramma. They're a team, and the children are winners for it.

If there's out-and-out rebellion—especially from an older child—invite prayer on the part of the entire family and other loved ones. Christ can give unexpected breakthroughs. Children, especially those who become born again, can learn that it's desirable to please Jesus.

Reflecting God

What's true for the child (and for every person) is that wrong thoughts about himself are rooted in wrong thoughts about God. His parents can help guide him into right thoughts.

Remember that our Father God "disciplines us for our good, that we may share his holiness" (Heb. 12:10). As earthly parents, we ask God to help us strive to be like him in disciplining our children.

Effective correction brings our sinful children into alignment with God's ways. We do that by reflecting God in our total approach to parenting. Take the matter of consistency, for example. Discipline must be consistent to be effective. The right kind of consistent discipline stems ultimately from *who God is*, because God is consistent, never changing.

Or take God's goodness. God is loving and holy and *good*. Ultimately, that means that you should aim for your children not to be "normal" (conforming to everyone else), but to be good. Aim for their goodness.

As my own children got older and would be heading out the door to some activity, their mother or I would say, "Don't be normal. Be good." Or we would ask, "What's the main thing?" and they would answer, "Be good."

In a moral sense, being normal in our culture is an unwise goal, because our culture itself is so broken, even vile. To tell your children to "act normal" is to invite them to look around to their peers to set the standard. To be normal is to be bad. And bad becomes worse. The trend is downward, so don't go with it.

Corrective discipline should especially reflect the love of God—the God who declares to us, "Those whom I love, I reprove and discipline" (Rev. 3:19).

I assume that you love your child. Knowing that you love your child, I'll pass along a two-word key to practicing correction: *Love confronts*. There's more to it, of course, but genuine love does not evade its responsibility to correct.

When I take a hoe to weed my garden, I love my garden, but I don't love everything that's growing there. When I correct my child, I love my child, but I don't love everything that's in my child. So corrections are called for.

Yes, God is good and loving—and God is also seriously holy. The goodness and severity of God together form a template for parents.

Good theology expands the soul, and we want our children to be children of a larger God—the God who is large enough to mean what he says, even when he says something as simple as *no*. There has been yes and no as long as there has been God. He affirms righteousness and denies falsehood.

My friends Ben and Amy Katterson understand well that good parenting reflects God. They bring three small boys (ages four and younger) to a weekly thirty-minute adult prayer meeting where those boys are quiet and obedient. I asked Ben and Amy to write down their secret as parents. Here's their response:

> One of our biggest parenting paradigms is that we are trying to be . . . a reflection to our children of how God is.
>
> He is faithful, so we strive to keep our word.
>
> He is kind, so we want to be gracious and gentle.
>
> He is generous, so we love to lavish our kids with good things.
>
> He is awesome and holy and sovereign over all creation, so we must not allow our children to disregard or belittle the authority that God has put over them—namely, parents.
>
> When God gives commands to his creatures, it is never for insignificant or capricious reasons. It is for our good, for our protection, for our abundant life. In our parenting, we want to reflect the same purposing for good when we give instructions or restrictions. And for the same reason— because obeying God is essential for knowing full joy and eternal abundance of life—when our children disobey or disregard our instructions, we find it important to address the failure and, when needed, follow up with discipline.
>
> God's words are utterly trustworthy. And so it is important that (as much as is humanly possible), our yes means yes and our no means no (James 5:12), without games of counting to ten or bluffing with impossible threats of what will happen if a child does not comply.
>
> Parenting is a tremendous responsibility and calling. We do it "as seems best" to us (Heb. 12:10), and so frequently we feel (and are) woefully inadequate to perceive

and respond rightly to the needs of the young hearts we are striving to shepherd. But what a kind Father we have, who supplies wisdom when we lack it (James 1:5), who set his love on us (1 John 3:1), and who has given the Savior and Mediator that our children need (1 Tim. 2:4–6).

Affirming Your Child

One of the most powerful reflections of God's kindness, generosity, and love will be the consistent affirmation you give your child.

Good correcting must be preceded by lots and lots of good affirmation. Saying yes first is crucial to expressing an effective no later. Consistent affirmation from parent to child will gain a hearing so that the parent's later correction will be heard.

The parent who's bent on practicing correction before first majoring on practicing affirmation is wise to take a hiatus from correction and first lay a groundwork of commending the commendable. Otherwise he'll become a tyrant, and his corrections will become off-putting and ineffective.

Say yes often. Then say no only when necessary. When you have first established many affirmations and permissions with your children, they are more apt to accept your "no" when they make unwise requests. A steady diet of wise affirmations establishes a helpful and healthy context in which subsequent restrictions and corrections are more easily swallowed.

In my book *Practicing Affirmation*, I assert that affirmation is a universal aspect of all relationships. Wise parents will seek a healthy proportionality of affirmations and denials, of yes and no. (*Practicing Affirmation* reflects my consistently affirming mom. This book, *Parenting with Loving Correction*, reflects my consistently correcting dad. Both are profoundly significant gifts of God.)

The overall backdrop and context of the total relationship with your children should be safe and affirming. Affirmation comes through with more than words. Parent with a smile and a twinkle in your eye. Stir in humor, laughing at yourself first. Yes, playfulness can be misplaced or get out of hand, but generally speaking, it lightens the mood for both children and adults.

Spend time interacting with the children when you're not demanding anything—just playing or exploring or making something together. I very much enjoyed taking our young children to the grocery store. Each small child would ride in a separate grocery cart, stacking groceries as I handed items to them. I turned over some of the decisions to them: Which soups shall we buy today? Which head of lettuce? How many buns do you think we'll need? We all looked forward to those trips to the store.

They also knew they didn't have permission to wander on their own around the store, or make fussy demands about what I should buy. They believed me when I told them that if necessary for correction, I'd walk them out of the store immediately and buy nothing. Because they knew from my past consistency that I meant what I said, I don't recall ever being in a store with them and having to follow through on that warning.

It was similar with baking. Oh, the happy adventures we had in the kitchen! My desire was for my children to be willing and able to attempt recipes. One way to learn to be comfortable in the kitchen is to participate with an adult who's also learning. So we donned aprons, and side by side at the counter, we would tackle the making of an apple pie or gingerbread men or a Tater Tot casserole. It was fun. It was work. Yes, they knew that they were to follow instructions and heed cautions about sharp objects and hot ovens. But mainly the adventures were playful. And delicious!

We were a team. We were learning. They knew I was the boss, but I didn't have to be bossy. And we learned together. (I'd never made an apple pie before.) We made happy memories.

As you work together with your children, don't expect their immediate perfection in the task at hand. Instead, commend incremental progress toward high standards. Commend your child for doing whatever portion of the task was performed properly. Celebrate that, then encourage further improvement.

Affirmation promotes encouragement. In Scripture, Paul mentions how encouragement goes along with exhortation in the pattern of fatherly guidance: "For you know how, like a father with his children, we *exhorted* each one of you and *encouraged* you and charged you to walk in a manner worthy of God, who calls you into his own kingdom and glory" (1 Thess. 2:11–12). Don't just correct, but exhort and encourage.

Likewise, parents can allow children to incrementally make larger and larger decisions, which in itself communicates affirmation. This will likely mean that parents incrementally reduce their quantity of no's. How rapidly can the no's be reduced? As soon as the child demonstrates consistently good decisions. The pace varies from child to child, and sometimes varies from season to season in the same child.

I've heard the stated rule "Affirm in public; correct in private." Maybe you've heard that too. Certainly, the aim of discipline is not to humiliate the child. So private correction has advantages. However, there can be significant benefits in allowing others—including other children—to see that there's a standard, and the standard will be maintained.

Public correction can (and should) be done graciously. When your Little Leaguer, while warming up to bat, is taking practice swings too close to his teammates, it's not rude or unkind to interject (quite publicly), "Junior, be careful of others.

Take your swings over there. Atta boy. Go get 'em, tiger. We're all for ya."

Standing up for singing during a church service, a mother was holding a clingy four-year-old who was too heavy for the mother to keep holding. Running out of strength, she slid the child down onto the pew, but the child clamored to be picked up, practically climbing onto the mother. The mother relented and again held the child, though she clearly showed the strain.

She could have simply placed her child on the pew, leaned over to make eye contact, calmly and wordlessly shook her head no, then turned to resume singing. But by caving in to the child, she wearied herself, rewarded the child's demands, put the child in charge, distracted worshipers seated behind them, and established a trajectory for her child's demandingness in the future. Simple correction can be—and sometimes should be—performed in public.

To *not* enforce standards when you're at restaurants or when Gramma comes or when you're in an unusually generous mood is to teach children that they don't have to obey when going out to eat or when Gramma visits or when you're whistling while you work. If they detect "safety zones" where your authority as a parent is not consistently applied, your children will behave differently in those zones—at the grocery store, in church, or wherever. In fact, children who discover that they won't be disciplined at the mall or the church foyer can become extremely defiant and obnoxious there.

This may mean that until you can achieve a relatively consistent measure of compliance, your child may have to forgo trips with you to restaurants or on airplanes or to the mall. You yourself may have to forgo some opportunities until compliance can be achieved. This is a high priority—for them, for you, for society, and for the church.

But take heart. In the vast majority of cases, compliance can be accomplished in a matter of days (not months or years).

Glorifying God

Biblical correction is motivated by and guided by a desire to glorify God: "Whatever you do, do all to the glory of God" (1 Cor. 10:31).

The church where I serve as pastor asks parents the following five questions. I think they're good reminders of what God-centered and God-glorifying parenting is all about:

1. Do you recognize these children as gifts of God and give heartfelt thanks for God's blessing?

2. Do you now dedicate your children to the Lord who gave them to you, surrendering all worldly claims upon their lives in the hope that they will belong wholly to God?

3. Do you pledge, as parents, that with God's fatherly help you will bring up your children in the discipline and instruction of the Lord, making every reasonable effort, with patience and love, to build the Word of God, the character of Christ, and the joy of the Lord into their lives?

4. Do you promise to provide, through God's blessing, for the physical, emotional, intellectual, and spiritual needs of your children, looking to your own heavenly Father for the wisdom, love, and strength to serve them and not use them?

5. Do you promise, God helping you, to make it your regular prayer that by God's grace your children will come to trust in Jesus Christ alone for the forgiveness of their sins and for the fulfillment of all his promises to them, even eternal life; and in this faith follow Jesus as Lord and obey his teachings?

We must always remember that our greater and higher aim is godly heart transformation in our children, not just behavioral correction. The ultimate reason for this aim is God's own focus on our hearts.

Godless, secular behaviorism obscures—even denies—the gospel. Our proper approach in corrective discipline means seeking our children's behavioral change with heart change always in view. Parents cannot create in a child's heart the kind of love that God can. He can create the love he commands. We can't transform the child's heart—but our own transformed hearts can shape behaviors that will benefit the child's future.

Correction doesn't save the soul. But salvation of the soul corrects—that is, it ushers in true heart transformation and a lifetime of change, by God's grace and will.

6

Speak Truth

Parents of young children have a divinely appointed task: *to speak*.

One of the words to speak is *no*.

Enforcing your no reflects the fact that correction is one of God's means to provide blessings of protection and direction. The crucial distinction between yes and no is important to your children, to you, to society, and to the church. That distinction is rooted in the importance of yes and no to God, who always means what he says.

Meaning what *we* say is a fundamental requirement for parents. There's a vital connection between what we say and what we do. Our actions and our words are indivisibly related.

In the garden, God said, "Do not . . ." He meant it, and proved it. So should we. When we say *don't* to our children, we should mean it and follow through.

God wired "mutual exclusivity" into the orderliness of the universe. No doesn't mean yes, and we do a disservice to children when we let them think it might. To not back up words with action is to foster confusion.

Truth Matters

"Peace if possible," Martin Luther is quoted as saying, "but truth at all costs." Truth matters—God makes that clear. We're told in Proverbs 23:23, "Buy truth, and do not sell it." Paul insists, "Having put away falsehood, let each one of you speak the truth" (Eph. 4:25).

Half-truths are whole lies. That's why a parent's no should mean no the first time; otherwise his word comes to be distrusted. Say it once. And mean it.

No one has to teach a child how to lie. Parental vacillations—not following through on our directives—will only further entrench the child's sinful bent toward truth suppression. A parent's equivocation leaves the child unprotected and more vulnerable to swallowing the postmodern notion (and lie) that there really is no absolute truth.

Because truth is integrative and applies to everything, then everything matters. *Especially* yes and no. Unfortunately, when some parents say no, or stop, or come here, they're just borrowing those words, trying them out, taking them for a test spin. They don't really mean what they're saying. What they mean is something like this: "I hope you'll agree with me, but I don't *really* expect you to obey me right now—first time and every time."

In fact, if their child *did* obey, such parents would be shocked. They themselves don't really believe their no means no. They have no decisive commitment to making their no mean this: "That's the end of the discussion until there's obedience. Once you've obeyed, *then* perhaps we can discuss these instructions."

Follow Through

I'm tempted to say, "If you ignore everything else in this book, follow this one pointer": *If we want our child to respond the first time we speak, we must demonstrate that we always mean it the first time.*

Being inconsistent will never produce the same results as being consistent. It's unlikely that any household standards you establish will have consequences as destructive to your children as failure to consistently uphold those standards. A child's future hangs on the parent's willingness to consistently follow through.

I don't intend in this book to map out in detail exactly when to say no or where to set boundaries. Rather, I wish you to underscore the vital importance of consistently meaning what you say—by actually enforcing the boundaries you've established.

Meaning what you say requires follow-through. This seems elementary to those parents (and dog trainers) who already embrace the practice of consistent reinforcement of yes and no. But to some of us, making no mean no can seem like a foreign language. If you're going to warn your child of what you'll do if he disobeys, then *do* what you say you'll do. If not, don't say it.

There's a difference between following through and badgering. Don't be a nag. Tell your child you won't nag. Then don't. Instead, act. The child needs to know he can trust you and your words. He finds security in knowing you'll do what you say you'll do—even if it's not what he'd *like* you to do. If you say you'll thump his finger if he touches that forbidden thing, then upon touching it, his fingers must be thumped—or you've gutted the meaning of your words, while also lessening your child's sense of security.

Hearing the word *no* can be painful for a child (or any of us, really). But our kind and loving God created pain for many reasons, one of them being a mechanism for instruction. When children consistently receive reasonable yet painful correction in response to their willful disobedience, they learn that there are behaviors to be avoided in the world.

If you make a pattern of delaying enforcement or just repeating your warnings without acting on them, you're teaching the child to disregard your initial instruction. You're making your words worthless. If he discovers that he can disregard your words without consequence, you're training your child to *not* pay attention.

When consistently demonstrating to your children that no means no, eventually you can drop the word almost altogether. You can simply give that "look" from across the room. Your child will know with certainty that if his or her behavior doesn't change, there will be a swift and sure consequence, which will not be enjoyable.

Meaning what you say means you don't keep repeating your warnings. One advantage of teaching a child to obey without multiple warnings will reveal itself later when he's alone and you aren't there to repeat the warning. One warning should suffice. If you've taught them when they're younger that one warning is all they'll get, then as they get older, one warning out in the world will be enough—one speed limit sign, one set of instructions on the prescription bottle, one caution on the appliance label.

A parent's wise *no*, wisely enforced, helps small children interpret life wisely. Enforcing *no* with young children provides important instruction and applies proper values and perspectives to life experiences. Some parents might instinctively understand this principle that if they issue a command, it's essential to enforce it. But then, because they don't want the burden of enforcement that's required, in many situations they'll simply opt *not* to give commands.

If you're one of those parents, then in all such situations you must acknowledge two things: (1) you imply that you're okay with *whatever* your child decides to do; (2) you have no ground for complaining about whatever he ends up doing. Choosing such a course—giving little or no direction—can result in not only fortifying negative behavior patterns in the child but also planting a violated conscience in the parent. Deep down, something tells you that you know better.

Eliminate Negative Reactions to Your "No"

Don't forget: the role of parenting is to *parent*. And in your God-given responsibilities as the parent, you must be after sheer obedience—meaning that your child obeys *because* he's told to, not because he necessarily agrees with the command. Sheer obedience demonstrates *actual* obedience, and not just agreement with the child's own preferred agenda.

Proper corrective action is what gives parental words their true meaning. Anger doesn't. Threats don't. Bargaining can't.

Bargaining's first "offer" is merely an initial invitation for a counterproposal. From the outset, bargaining assumes that the first proposal won't be the one that finally gets carried out. So don't be lured into an argument with your child when it comes to correction. Don't bargain, and don't debate.

To debate young children is to expect them to ask the right questions—which is dubious, for they may not yet see the real issues. Children are not adults. They can be insightful about some things, and we can indeed learn from them. But when they debate your instructions, this demonstrates rebellion, not insight. When you've determined the right command to give your child in any situation, then his number of options is one: obey. His number of permissible excuses is zero. If you forbid the child to do something, your "no" shouldn't mean compliance later, but right now.

When you engage in an argument with your child about why he should obey you, you relegate yourself to a hopeless search for better arguments—arguments that will satisfy your child.

But your child doesn't want to engage in rational discussion. He attaches no weight to being convinced or proven wrong. He just wants to have his way. He knows it's a war of wills.

When you apply corrective discipline, you don't need to fish for proofs or arguments to back up your rules or standards. You already have what you need: parental jurisdiction, under God. You're also bigger than your child, a God-given advantage you'll have for only a season.

Don't get lured onto the why-go-round. If your child has to be sold on what he must do, he's not submitting or obeying; he's negotiating. "Spinning" your commands to your children will backfire. If they spin into obedience, they've learned spin, which isn't at all what Jesus calls for. What he calls for is obedience, which includes letting yes be yes and no be no.

As I've written elsewhere, "no" doesn't mean the child should try a little harder, whine a little louder, throw a bigger hissy fit, or put up arguments.[1] Don't permit or excuse sassing. To do so damages both child and parent—the one sassing and the one being sassed. The moment there's sass, the issue becomes the sassing, *not* the topic they're being sassy about (bedtime, eating, homework, whatever).

Like sassing, whining from your child is another response to your commands that should be unacceptable. Vicki and I used to say to our young children (even up through their teenage years), "When you ask for something, we'll consider it. If you whine, permission is automatically denied, and the answer to your request will be no."

As time went on, whenever we encountered their whiny tone, we would simply ask, "Are you whining?" Their tone and demeanor changed, becoming civil and respectful as they

---

1. Sam Crabtree, "Parents, Let Your 'No' Be 'No,'" Desiring God website, October 16, 2013, https://www.desiringgod.org/articles/parents-let-your-no-be-no.

proceeded with their appeal. They eliminated their own whining, because they knew we would keep our word. No would mean no.

Back talk, stalling, and evasion are all forms of disobedience—just like arguing, sassing, and whining. Don't allow those things; *act*. Get obedience first, *then* consider any discussion, explanations, and appeals. We as parents should not feel obligated to explain our every command in detail *before* we expect our child's obedience. The parent who persists in such explaining is not promoting the child's obedience. In fact, that parent is placing himself under the authority of the child.

Such parenting issues no commands, only suggestions. All the authority remains with the child, leaving him to essentially conclude, "Mom, your agenda will become mine only if I happen to like it. The schedule is mine, the goals are mine. You're my vending machine, and if you don't work well, I'll shove you out of the way until I need you." To your child, his own desires are far more important than your desires.

I remember in high school being at my friend Doug's house for supper. As we were discussing an upcoming event, one of Doug's siblings said, "Mom, can we go?"

Doug's father responded calmly, "Ask your question to me, because I have an answer—and it is no." That was the end of the discussion. Without yelling or threatening, he decisively acted on his parental jurisdiction. At his house, no meant no. That house, as I remember, was a very healthy household, a fun place to be. There was a lot of laughter—and a lot of reverence for God.

Communicate Certainty

Enforcing your word as a parent must not be random—enforced on one occasion but not another. Random and capricious enforcement not only introduces chaos, but also opens a way for the child's heart to harbor bitterness. Your statements lose their meaning if they aren't steadily reaffirmed and reinforced.

Children are helped when they understand the *certainty* of correction. Certainty is not severity. Certainty is more effective than severity. As a boy, I knew that if I got in trouble at school, it was a certainty that I would be in trouble when I got home. That knowledge affected my behavior at school.

Once a command—sit in your chair, kennel the dog, give the toy back to your brother—is met with the child's disobedience, the issue *immediately* becomes the child's defiance—not the chair, the dog, or the toy. The issue is no longer bedtime or mealtime manners or whatever you were seeking to correct.

When your child is not compliant, administer clear-cut consequences the first time, every time. Don't allow your child to pull back his hand, run away, scream, or kick. Children benefit from learning the certainty of justice promptly administered. This is far more effective than your nagging, hollering, or bullying, or any response that's given impulsively, angrily, or whimsically.

Imagine, for example, that your kids are fighting over a toy. "Stop that, or else," you respond. You then back this up with the threat of some vague severity: "No dessert for a year"; "I'll ground you till you're twenty-one." But far more effective is a simple certainty: "One more outcry, and I'll take away that toy." Then couple that warning with your ironclad follow-through.

A corollary of the certainty principle is to never make excuses for your child's disobedience. When a child throws a fit, it won't do to respond by saying, "He's so tired." That may well be true, but the root problem is that he's being naughty. Being tired is no excuse for behavior that you've identified as unacceptable. Tired adults may not excuse themselves for committing sin, and neither is it wise to excuse naughtiness in tired children. Even when tired, children can learn that certain behaviors will earn them painful consequences.

Furthermore, if children discover that their tiredness grants them excuses, they'll take advantage of tiredness as a license. To rationalize and excuse inappropriate outbursts because the child is tired or ill or disappointed or young or "just expressing his emotions," is leaving unchecked a form of disrespect that will only grow as he increasingly tests you to see how far you'll let him go. If you make excuses for your child, he'll learn to make his own excuses. He'll polish excuse-making as a craft.

Children who are given a command will sometimes respond with excuses like these: "It's too hard"; "I don't *like* it"; "No one else has to do it"; "I don't feel well." Typically, such excuses are directly opposite of the Christlike character qualities that are wise to develop while young. Like these:

- Diligence and effort in the face of strenuous difficulty
- Endurance when the urge rises to give up, especially when experiencing weariness
- Self-control when you're thinking "I don't feel like it" or "I don't *want* to"
- Determination when triumph isn't achieved right away
- Stewardship when losing track of things.
- Attentiveness when being distracted; redirecting attention to priorities
- Responsibility when assigned a task
- Deference when in another's jurisdiction and under that person's authority

When we rigorously and consistently follow through, then follow-through becomes less and less necessary. The parent's corrective discipline tends to result in more enjoyable and reliable interactions with the child. If applied early, wisely, and consistently, the rod of correction eventually seldom needs to be applied.

Consistent enforcement of stable household rules is a kindness and establishes justice. Carefully establish your boundaries and limits and maintain them consistently. Then be prepared: your limits *will* be tested. Children test our limits to see if we mean them.

Whatever and wherever those limits are, our children will benefit from them. Remember, however, that standards and expectations will vary from household to household. One family may have significantly different rules from another, and yet in both homes, children can function peacefully—as long as parents are consistent in enforcing all the standards in their particular home.

For example, some parents let their children stay up much later than other parents do. That's fine. But once you establish the time for bed, or say, "Get your jammies on," you must correct any violations. The point is to be consistent once you've established what behaviors you will or won't accept. Without consistent enforcement, the child is left with just your good or bad moods. It's dysfunctional when a child realizes that a rule is whatever pleases the adult at the moment. The ground is always shifting underfoot.

So don't be capricious about rules. Either enforce them, or cancel them altogether.

Be Flexible

All this is not to say there's never a time and a place for discussion, appeals, and negotiation when it comes to corrective discipline.

Wise parents are flexible. But wise flexibility is like a dancer around a maypole: the dancer moves gracefully with her colorful streamer attached to the maypole, but the maypole stays put.

You can and should have open discussions with your children about everything, welcoming their observations and inviting their suggestions. I believe children should be allowed and invited to express their feelings—without sassiness, back talk, or delayed disobedience. And only *after* they have complied with what you have instructed them to do. *Any* instruction or command or prohibition from you requires obedience and enforcement.

Allow your child to make an appropriate appeal. But be wise. These appeals can be genuine attempts by your child to help you see something you've overlooked, but they can also be delay tactics, evasive debates, and cagey red herrings.

If the child responds negatively after you have heard his appeal and denied his request—crying, whining, arguing—assure him that even worse consequences will follow, swiftly and surely. Or, as my dad (for whom I thank God) would say, "I'll give you something to cry about." Only after there's compliance with your rules and standards should you permit your child to question them with respectful deference.

Generally, it's easier to reverse a no than a yes. However, be cautious about doing too many reversals. If you determine that a rule is wrong, apologize and cancel it. But impulsively and frequently changing your rulings, *especially* in response to your child's defiance and whining, has a detrimental impact on his confidence in your consistency.

Allow your child to discuss with you any standard for his or her behavior at home or out in the world—for church, for school, for dating, for driving, for clothing, for tattoos, for piercings, for social media, or whatever's on your child's mind. Voluntarily research your answers to the more involved questions your child asks. This will demonstrate that you're interested in his or her interests, not just your own. It builds a friendly context for if and when the time comes for correction.

Deal with Your Anger

When no doesn't always mean no the first time, frustration mounts, and that frustration can erupt in parental anger and overcoercion at one end of the spectrum, or giving up and capitulation on the other. Both of those wrong responses are terribly harmful. But let's talk especially for a moment about anger.

The effort to speak truth to our children might be taken by some parents as an excuse not to control the anger they sometimes feel when their children are disobedient. But this is extremely unwise. Anger is dangerous. There's never an appropriate time for parents to yell or scream shamingly at their children, or whack them around. The rod of correction is best held by a discerning hand that is at once both firm and gentle— not an unrestrained, angry, uncontrolled hand.

My friend Gil McConnell, a pastor for family discipleship at Bethlehem Baptist Church in Minneapolis, wrote this to me:

> Some people do not realize they have anger issues until they are parents. And then, all of a sudden, buttons are pushed and tempers flare. Some moms and dads think they need to be "firm" to get their point across, but their version of "firm" is really an expression of anger. Therefore, parents should earnestly pray that our meek Lord Jesus would root out unholy, underlying, and overtly angry expressions with their children in discipline and daily interactions. Our anger provokes anger in our children, and we do not want to do that (Eph. 6:4).

When I correct my child in anger, these are some of the consequences of that anger:

- I lose control of myself. Anger can elicit excessive consequences, piling up additional regrets. Oh, the regrets that have been precipitated by my mouth! Correction should be reasonable, not excessive.
- I model poorly for my child. My anger can provoke anger in the child, and the Bible insists that we're not to do that. "Fathers, do not provoke your children, lest they become discouraged" (Col. 3:21); "Fathers, do not provoke your children to anger, but bring them up in the discipline and instruction of the Lord" (Eph. 6:4). That verse is a particular application of a much broader principle applying to everyone's speech, in all our relationships: "A soft answer turns away wrath, but a harsh word stirs up anger" (Prov. 15:1).
- I exalt folly. "Whoever is slow to anger has great understanding, but he who has a hasty temper exalts folly" (Prov. 14:29).
- I cause more sin. "A man of wrath stirs up strife, and one given to anger causes much transgression" (Prov. 29:22). I generally makes things worse in my anger, fostering contention. "A hot-tempered man stirs up strife, but he who is slow to anger quiets contention" (Prov. 15:18).
- I essentially disqualify myself from friendship with my children, because of the danger that they'll adopt my anger. "Make no friendship with a man given to anger, nor go with a wrathful man, lest you learn his ways and entangle yourself in a snare" (Prov. 22:24–25).
- I produce unhealthy physical ramifications—hypertension (high blood pressure), stomach knots, grinding of teeth, and more.

Anger—in the parent or in the child—rarely equals power for doing good, and usually ends up being destructive. If necessary, take time to cool down. If you do lash out, ask for forgiveness immediately.

While you're taking time to cool down your anger, what else can you proactively and intentionally do? The biggest struggle in the angry moment is not what to do about your feelings, but what to do about your *thoughts*—specifically, your expectations. Anger is virtually always a by-product of expecting one thing and getting another. When our circumstances don't match what we were expecting, the result is negative emotions—disappointment, loneliness, sadness. Our focus in such a moment may easily tend toward anger.

Emotions stem not so much from our circumstances, but from our interpretation of those circumstances. My anger is an opportunity to identify my idolatrous thinking—I think I deserve circumstances other that what God has delivered at the moment. My anger is an opportunity to grow in sanctification and self-control.

So the key to overcoming anger is to yield to God in that moment. Yield expectations. If expectations align with reality—with what God is up to in that moment—anger will dissipate pretty quickly and be replaced with humble gratitude and renewed focus.

I can imagine a sincere parent who is reading up to this point saying something like, "I'm feeling like I need some words of grace to me as a parent. I can identify myself as a failure in just about every single paragraph. Please offer me some encouragement and hope." That parent is me. Failure is my middle name. Other than God, defective parents are the only kind on earth. So we lean in to him for another fresh start, for enabling grace, for reassurance that in his infinitely wise and loving providence he assigned these dear children to us (with our flaws and fail-ings) *for their good*, just like he gave *us* flawed parents for our ultimate eventual good. He is not done refining our children or us! He is cheering us on while we all avail ourselves of his en-abling grace to become decreasingly defective in our parenting . . . in the strength he supplies.

7

Reward Obedience, Not Disobedience

A friend of ours stopped by our house with her elementary school–aged son. As she stood chatting with my wife, Vicki, the boy climbed onto the back of the couch.

"Neil, get down off the couch," the mother said.

The boy sat there unmoved as she continued to chat.

"Neil, get down off the couch," she repeated, then kept talking with Vicki about other things.

The boy visibly stiffened his resolve. On his face and in his posture, you could see it: of all the things in the world Neil could do, he wasn't going to get down from that couch.

The game was on.

"Neil, if you don't get down off that couch, Sam and Vicki aren't going to like you."

Frankly, that's irrelevant. To Neil, whether we like him or not was immaterial. (We like him. Years later I officiated at his wedding.)

The boy stayed put. Neil's defiance had become the issue—not the couch, and not Sam and Vicki. The mother started digging in her purse. "Here, Neil, I'll give you this candy bar if you get down off the couch." When she pulled out the candy bar, he hopped down and fetched the candy bar.

Checkmate.

Mom loses.

Get this: she may *think* she's rewarding him for his obedience. Actually, she's *paying* him to disobey her. Guess what she's going to get lots more of?

Neil was obeying not his mother, but his sweet tooth. And the mother was catering to that.

Think back to the illustration that opened this book—of the harried mother in the grocery store aisle shouting "You're wasting time!" to her howling and whining boys who demand that she buy what they want.

Observe that her unruly sons know she has authority. Each purchase depends on her approval. She's the one with the money. The question is, how will that poor beleaguered mom use that authority?

Observe also that the boys don't whine to anyone else in the store. Why? Because they've learned that it works only with Mom. It gets them what they want from her. They don't whine to anyone else because that doesn't work. They've learned that no other adult will capitulate to this naughty behavior.

Although the mother says no to most of their demands, she occasionally says, "Okay." *She rewards the whining!* And the boys conclude, in effect, "Whining works, if we keep it up long enough and loud enough."

If you're startled at the thought that you might actually be rewarding rebellion, whining, sassiness, and disobedience in your child, keep reading. None of us wants to be a parent that rewards the wrong thing in our child. This chapter can help you avoid that.

Rewards Are Part of God's Design

Once more, let's revisit our working definition for corrective discipline.

Corrective discipline means:

(1) Identifying actions or attitudes of your child that are unacceptable when weighed against clear and explicit standards—then

(2) acting promptly and decisively to move your child in the direction of compliance with those standards.

What does "acting decisively" look like? The main kind of decisive action parents must engage in is rewarding obedience in their children, not disobedience. Here's a principle that God himself wired into the kingdoms of beasts and human beings: rewarded behaviors tend to be repeated, while behaviors that aren't rewarded (or that receive negative reinforcement) tend to reoccur less often. Rewards provide a payoff, which strengthens the likelihood for behaviors to become a habit or pattern.

God himself delights in using rewards. In fact, "whoever would draw near to God must believe that he exists and that he *rewards* those who seek him" (Heb. 11:6). So use rewards. Use them promptly. God has embedded this into the way the universe operates. Our children's spiritual hearts reside in bodies that we can reward—or punish—in order to shape behavior patterns.

Let's review—from a child's perspective—this principle that rewarded behaviors are more likely to be repeated. From the child's point of view, the goal of his behavior—the desirable result—is simply "getting my own way." The more successful your child is at getting his own way through misbehaving, the more likely he is to misbehave again and again.

For example, kids generally like attention from adults. Children who feel ignored by their parents may conclude that negative attention is better than none at all. When they gain attention by complaining, you'll get more complaining. On the other hand, a pattern of obedience is also strengthened in the child if the pattern is appropriately rewarded and praised. God has made our minds and hearts to work that way.

Some parents are uncomfortable with the idea of rewards. It seems like bribery. But note this helpful distinction: *rewards* are granted for *good* behavior (faithful work earns a paycheck, a touchdown puts points on the scoreboard, a skillful performance generates applause); bribes are an attempt to hide *bad* behavior (unscrupulous or illegal activity, such as insurance scams, false inspections, etc.).

Other parents may hesitate to use rewards because it seems to belong in the realm of secular behaviorism, which obscures and even denies the gospel. I don't advocate secular behaviorism. However, behavioral methods—rewards and punishments— *can be* means toward good spiritual ends—in particular, they can draw the child's attention to the gospel.

In God's design, wise rewards have a reinforcing effect, and wise punishments have a deterring effect. Though I much prefer using positive reinforcement, when that isn't adequate, strategically and consistently applied negative reinforcement can work wonders.

Who's Training Whom?

Children aren't the only ones susceptible to behavior reinforcement. Children can train their *parents*. A child may not come right out and say it, but the thinking goes like this: "I'll stop whining when you give me my way." We give him his way. He stops whining, which is what we wanted. But *he* is now in control. The whining has not been eliminated; it has actually been established as a means of controlling the adults.

If that (or something like it) has been your experience, then don't keep doing what hasn't been working. You might protest by thinking, "My approach must work, because he stopped whining when I gave him what he wanted." No, he only temporarily relented from his whining until the next thing comes along that he wants. Then it's back to whining.

We teach kids to whine—or to delay in obeying or to cry loudly or to argue with us. How? By rewarding it. Parents often unwittingly reinforce undesirable behaviors and weaken the very behaviors they value.

I observed a mother whose little boy was defiantly disobeying her instructions, so she scooped him up and playfully smooched him and cuddled him. If that child enjoys cuddling with mommy, she just rewarded his defiance. She should expect more of it to come. If you, the parent, did something that got you hugged and kissed, you'd likely repeat the behavior too! When your child is naughty is not the time to cuddle and smooch him.

The child's "training" of the parent also happens with his delayed obedience. The reason your child continues his misbehavior until you're angry, or you count to ten, or you get up out of your chair, is that he has learned your pattern. He has learned how to identify when you really mean what you claim to mean. Worse, if he knows his persistence in delayed obedience might result in your offering a reward that heretofore hasn't been offered, you've taught him to delay until the terms of the reward have been specified.

He's no dummy. Why obey you automatically when he can instead delay, ignore, fuss, whine, or throw a tantrum and get rewarded for it? You think you're rewarding his obedience; he knows you're rewarding his disobedience.

If we don't respond to disobedience until we become frustrated and then raise our voice, the children learn that they don't have to mind until the decibels climb. *Everyone* will be far happier if you say things once (and only once), and then follow through.

More Dynamics of Rewards

This next observation is important. Read carefully. If a behavior has become entrenched because it has been rewarded over time, then when you stop rewarding it, the behavior will eventually extinguish—but before it does, *it will increase*. The bad behavior will actually spike.

If you try to extinguish whining in your child, you'll at first get more whining. But don't cave in. If you do, you'll just reward the *increase* in whining, and increased whining is what you'll get more of. By allowing wrong behavior to accomplish the child's desired result, that wrong behavior (whining, fussing, tantrum) is thereby rewarded and hence strengthened, not weakened.

The good news is that *any* entrenched pattern of misbehavior in the child that has been misguidedly reinforced by the parent's rewards *can* be eliminated if those rewards are withheld long enough. And extinction of that learned misbehavior can be hastened with negative reinforcement. If a child persists in doing something inappropriate—whether outright naughty, like defying you, or just ill-fitting, like being overly rambunctious—you'll help him stop if you respond to that behavior with a swift, sure consequence he doesn't like.

This is critical: don't cave in! If you make one single exception, you risk undoing all the progress you've made with the child. This is a zero exception policy you must establish for yourself, in the strength God supplies.

Another dynamic that's built into rewards is that they're most effective when granted immediately. Time moves more slowly for children than it does for us. That's especially true for small children. So the power of any reward you offer is weakened over time.

As you go shopping, you tell your child, "If you behave in the store, I'll give you a treat when we get home." That can be like saying he can have a cookie in twenty or thirty years. "When we get home" can be an eternity to a child, an irrelevance. By the time you get home, the child may have lost all connection to what's being reinforced. In fact, it's *not* being reinforced. To effectively reinforce the behaviors of youngsters, rewards must be immediate. Before issuing a command, it is essential to first ask yourself if you're going to be willing to enforce it immediately.

The mature person delays gratification when such delay is warranted—waiting for a payday, for supper, for sex. The immature person doesn't do that. The ability to delay is a feature of maturity, and isn't present in the immature. So it stands to reason that your immature child will resist going along with your directives that require delay. Waiting until after dinner for a cookie isn't a decision an immature person makes. And when someone else makes that decision for him, he won't like it (though much later, when he matures, he may look back with appreciation).

Rewards need not be material in nature (snacks, money, a new toy, etc.). In fact, nonmaterial reinforcement should start early and permeate the entire span of the parent-child relationship—with words, hugs, smiles, nods of approval, and the child's own clear conscience, which you helped him achieve.

Meanwhile, keep reading; we'll be getting even more practical in the third part of this book.

Part 3

GETTING PRACTICAL

8

Before You Correct

Wise discipline for your children begins prior to any actual incident of misbehavior. The freedom to practice correction wisely and effectively comes from understanding the essentials we looked at earlier, plus rightly preparing yourself and your family in light of those essentials.

Prepare Yourself

Before disciplining children, discipline yourself. Jesus would put it this way: get the log out of your own eye.

Do you model a Christlike heart and character? For aiming effectively at your child's heart attitudes, it's essential to examine attitudes in your own heart. Our adult lives must reflect what we wish to inculcate in our children.

Do you model dying to self (delay of gratification)? One of the most effective ways to teach children to embrace "no" is to embrace it ourselves. We must model self-discipline. An essential element of character is the ability and willingness to say no to temptations, to urges, to excesses. Do your children hear you saying no to your desire for second helpings, or to that impulse purchase?

Examine your own personal modeling. Are you free from hypocrisy? Kids have hypocrisy antennae, and they bristle inside when they perceive you want them to "do what I say, not what I do." For example, do you cheerfully accept your own disciplinary punishments—such as parking tickets? Do you model cheerful obedience to authorities? Is your conscience clear? Do what's necessary (no matter how painful) to make it so. Follow Paul's example: "I always take pains to have a clear conscience toward both God and man" (Acts 24:16).

Humble Yourself for the Work of Discipline

Good discipline of children is a loving service rendered to them, but when performed in sinful pride, the children can sense something is awry. It can shipwreck the whole operation.

Pride takes many forms in parents. It causes timid or lazy parents to exacerbate problems by avoidance. Pride moves overly permissive parents to delay and derail discipline by accommodation. Pride gets placating parents to disembowel "no" by compromise. Pride causes harsh parents to wound others through triumphalism: "Don't talk to *me* that way, Buster!"

It's not about you; it's about God.

Pride brings destruction. "God opposes the proud" (James 4:6). If there's anything a parent doesn't need, it's God's resistance. So how do we humble ourselves for the parental responsibility of correctively disciplining our children? Here are a few strategic ways.

Most importantly, *pray for God's help in your parenting.* "You do not have," Scripture tells us, "because you do not ask" (James 4:2). Ask for God's help.

God is the main worker. Asking him to work is not some technique, but explicit, conscious dependence upon the main actor to act. Ask him to help you, grow you, and improve your parenting.

Ask God to show you how you might be fostering or rewarding your child's disobedience. Ask him for fresh ways to correct and encourage your child. (And in love for your neighbors, ask God to help your friends raise *their* children.)

Beware of placing confidence in mere techniques. Remember: "It is God who works in you, both to will and to work for his good pleasure" (Phil. 2:13).

Ask God specifically to guide your tongue, so that you mean what you say and say what you mean. "Let your speech always be gracious, seasoned with salt, so that you may know how you ought to answer each person" (Col. 4:6).

Depend on God's enabling grace. Rely on that grace to:

- control your own attitudes and tongue.
- overcome your own anger.
- conform *you* to the image of Jesus.
- transform your children into believers.
- temper any expectations that you'll have perfect children by reading a book, or by applying your own good intentions.

"Be filled with the Spirit" (Eph. 5:18). Parents need all of the Holy Spirit's ninefold fruit: "The fruit of the Spirit is love, joy, peace, patience, kindness, goodness, faithfulness, gentleness, self-control . . ." (Gal. 5:22–23). Notice *joy* in that list. Make sure that in the Spirit, your own heart is pursuing delight in God.

Earnestly pursue wisdom and love, as biblically understood. Be diligent to learn wise correction. Good parenting is never automatic. Apply yourself wholeheartedly to these things. Work in the strength God supplies. Your diligence can mean writing down the most important standards you want to enforce in your home. That's nothing new. Back in England in the early 1700s, Susanna Wesley—who gave birth to nineteen children, including John and Charles Wesley—laid down sixteen rules for her role as parent. Here are a few of them:[1]

4. Subdue self-will in a child. . . .
6. Require all to be still during Family Worship.
7. Give them nothing that they cry for, and only that when asked for politely.
9. Never allow a sinful act to go unpunished.
11. Comment and reward good behavior.
12. Any attempt to please, even if poorly performed, should be commended.
16. Teach children to fear the rod.

Prepare Your Family

Besides preparing yourself, you'll also want to prepare your family and your home environment for wise discipline.

Most importantly, pray for your children. Ask God to make your children receptive to correction. Pray for them by name. Ask God to bind the Enemy of your children. Ask God to put a hedge of protection around them. Point with thanksgiving to the good work of God in your children already. They're made in his image, and he's at work in them.

Explore and apply the Bible with your children. Read it to them and with them. Invite them to read it to you. Meditate together on it. Be alert to observe in the Scriptures where people

1. "16 House Rules by Susannah Wesley (John Wesley's Mom)," Raising Godly Children website, http://www.raisinggodlychildren.org/2011/03/16-house-rules-by-susannah-wesley-john-wesleys-mom.html.

experienced disciplinary correction. Talk about such stories together. (Expose your children also to good biographies that include experiences of being disciplined, such as the life stories of Helen Keller, Adam Clarke, or the boyhoods of George Washington and Frederick Douglass.)

And remember again the pattern of parental discipline set by God the Father himself: "For the moment all discipline seems painful rather than pleasant, but *later it yields the peaceful fruit of righteousness* to those who have been trained by it" (Heb. 12:11). Aim for your child's peace and righteousness. Under God's fatherly care, confirm to your children their belongingness and acceptance in your family. Lay down a robust foundation of affirmation, consistently commending each child for the good things he or she does.

Know Each Child Well

Learn your children. One of the discoveries that continually impresses parents is how different siblings can be. Not all children respond the same to certain forms of correction. Each of them is to be disciplined, but the discipline is to be customized to fit each child's wiring.

Be aware of your need to customize correction. One child thinks it's the end of the world if you take away the Legos, while his sibling is barely fazed. And don't punish all the children just because one child mouthed off or threw a tantrum.

Wisdom distinguishes between training children in mere mechanical robot-like obedience and training them in their God-given bent, giftedness, and individual personality. Tailor discipline to the child. Rewards for a specific child must actually be rewarding from that child's perspective; likewise, assigned punishments must be aversive from each child's perspective.

Parents must also proactively inspect their children's behavior. If certain attitudes are desirable (kindness, thankfulness, cheerfulness), then teach those attributes, model them, and actively be on the lookout for them. If you tell a child, "Share your game with your brother," immediately look to see if the initial steps to compliance are being taken. Then extend a reward: "Thanks for sharing with your brother. Good job! Your sharing makes him happy, and it pleases me—and God." The more you affirm good patterns, the less you'll need to correct bad ones.

Plan Ahead

Remember that good intentions and good discipline are not the same. Plan ahead for what you'll do in response to the kinds of disobedience most likely to occur in your family, and inform everyone of your plan. This is far superior to waiting until you can't take it anymore, and you erupt with a reaction conceived in the moment, on the fly. Are bedtimes combative? Plan for them. Is going to a restaurant war? Plan ahead.

Plan by assuming the worst will happen, and map out what you'll do if it occurs. Communicate the plan to the child in advance. Then, if the worst happens, carry out your plan. If the worst doesn't happen, your disciplinary communication with your child is already bringing benefits.

A lot of misbehavior can be headed off before correction ever becomes necessary. How? By trying to avoid circumstances that can typically give rise to misbehavior, such as overtiredness or too much sugar. Be alert for influences in your home that can easily trigger your children's misbehavior. For example, materialism can foster a sense of entitlement and impoliteness in your children. If we overindulge a child's consumer impulses ("But I *want* one!"), we tilt them toward becoming demanding instead of grateful and contented. Large gifts can create an "encore problem"—an appetite for even larger gifts, and dissatisfaction with smaller gifts. It can fuel a child's drift away from gratitude toward an expectation of entitlement. You may need to seriously address the degree of materialism in yourself and your family.

Communicate Expectations Clearly

When my daughters Dawn and Mandi were in their midtwenties, I asked them to look back over the years of their upbringing and answer this question: "What's important in parenting?" Their answer included this: *Establish consistent boundaries.*

Clearly and specifically define your family's rules and boundaries before enforcing them. "You may ride your tricycle up the sidewalk to that tree, and down the sidewalk to the Olsons' mailbox, but no further. Understand?" Clearly defined rules and boundaries are like reliable fences that establish comfort zones.

It's best to keep family rules to a minimum. Your aim is for minimum rules, but consistent, instant enforcement of the rules you make. And zero idle threats.

In some situations it's wise to let children set their own rules. Wisely transfer more and more responsibility to your child for making his own decisions, and make that transfer explicit: "From now on, Jimmy, you decide whether we have oranges or grapefruit for breakfast; it's your call."

You want fewer rules, but there's a time and a place for adding new ones. I recently had the delightful opportunity to be "solo grandpa" for four of my grandchildren (ages eleven, eight, six, and four) for four-and-a-half days, twenty-four hours a day. Each morning I made sure they were dressed, fed them breakfast, and dropped the older ones off at their schools before I began keeping the four-year-old engaged all day with me. In the afternoon I received them home again from school and provided snacks. In the evenings I made supper. I made sure they did their Scripture memory and their homework, and got baths. I told bedtime stories and read the Bible with them.

In the process of all this, I decided to implement a new rule: yes to snacks after getting home from school, but no snacks after 4:00 p.m. until after supper.

The first day of this new rule I heard the predictable chorus of moaning: "I'm sooo hungry!" But I persisted. The second day, only one child said, "Grandpa, I'm hungry." To which I simply said, "We'll have supper in a little while." By day three, no one said anything. And they did a better job of eating supper. And we had enjoyable conversations at the dinner table.

Be committed to consistency in enforcing your family's rules and boundaries. Your child will learn to operate peacefully within the limits you've established as long as you don't constantly redefine those limits. Remain consistent. Don't keep shifting his boundaries. Don't keep moving the line he's not supposed to cross.

Every time a child steps over that line, you correct. But if you keep moving that line—one day you let him have a cookie before dinner, but the next day you don't—then he no longer knows where the line is. He'll bounce all over the place, constantly testing your limits, because he's never quite sure where they are.

You don't want to be a tyrant. Tyranny is marked by surprise legislation, laws invented on the spot, laws rapidly changing without opportunity for appeal, and harsh punishment for violations. Despots make up rules on impulse. In contrast, good parents make known their expectations in advance, and make them clear. Stable guidelines and behavioral limits foster a sense of security.

Be Clear about Consequences

Be clear also about establishing the consequences of disobedience. Your readiness for the moment when correction is required includes knowing your options. Several forms of corrective response are available to parents, like these:

Solitude. "Go sit in that chair until I come and get you."

Removal. "Since you're fighting over it, we're putting that toy away."

Restraint. Scoop up the child and pull him away from the skirmish; physically carry him to the bathtub; take away the toy from his grip.

Natural consequences. The top of the child's ice cream cone falls off into the gravel. "That's why we try to be careful, buddy. I guess we'll just have to enjoy what's left in the cone."

Appeal to conscience. "Do you think your behavior pleases Jesus?" "Is this the way a young man should behave?"

Logical consequences. "We won't get you a bicycle until you consistently put your tricycle away each day."

For a while, our young children had a pet cat . Our arrangement with the kids went something like this (a blend of logical consequences and removal): "We're glad you enjoy cat ownership. The cat is yours. Since it's your cat, the cat chores are your chores. I'm willing and happy to fill in for you in performing the cat chores if you're away—at summer camp, or a sleepover at Gramma's, for instance. But if you're not away, and we find that the cat chores aren't being performed, well, I don't need cat chores. Is my meaning clear?" (Implication: I'll take your lack of faithful performance of the cat chores as an indication that you no longer want a cat, and I'll get rid of it without further discussion. *This* is the discussion. This is the warning. Now, enjoy the cat.)

One thing I recommend to *not* use as punishment is necessary household chores. Those chores then take on negative associations, instead of being seen as something that mature people do. We want children to find satisfaction in pulling their weight on the team. So when they're contributing to the functioning of the household, don't equate that to punishment. If you make taking out the garbage a punishment, they'll think it's something only naughty people do.

What about Spanking?

Another form of corrective response is spanking. Because spanking is controversial, it calls for careful discussion in this book.

A widely held yet mistaken assumption today is that any kind of corporal punishment for children is necessarily injurious and only teaches them violence. That assumption doesn't align with the Bible, where Solomon in his wisdom wrote, "Whoever spares the rod hates his son, but he who loves him is diligent to discipline him" (Prov. 13:24). Discipline done well—*including* the wise, loving, just, and certain application of the rod—is good for a child. It helps him bring his stubborn will under control. Left out of control, that stubborn, childish willfulness is beastly, which is no good for the individual or for anyone around him.

While it's sadly and tragically true that parents can be abusive, tyrannical, oppressive, harsh, and worse, discipline— including a spanking rightly administered—is in the best interest of the child. Just because a practice is performed wrongly doesn't mean the practice itself is wrong.

Selective spankings can be very loving indeed. The most happy, peaceful homes I've witnessed are those where spanking is done well (which means, for one thing, that spanking is selective and rare). Much less peaceful by far are those homes where spanking has been abused or abandoned. Corporal punishment in the hands of a loving, prudent, decisive, firm-but-gentle parent is not abuse. Failure to correct *is* abuse.

Accidents and mistakes are not cause for spankings, which should be reserved for instances involving conscious defiance. When a child's defiance is clearly intentional and his disobedience is deliberate—he consciously arches his back, grits his teeth, shouts, or spits at you—correction must speak decisively, consistently, firmly, and lovingly. Such a response from the parent does *not* create aggression; rather, it stems the aggression *already* in the child.

Correction, including appropriate corporal punishment, helps the child learn to control impulses and to cooperate with benevolent authorities in the moment and for the remainder of his life.

Not only the child's behavior, but the child's soul is at stake: "Do not withhold discipline from a child; if you strike him with a rod, he will not die. If you strike him with the rod, you will save his soul from Sheol" (Prov. 23:13–14).

And wise application of the rod sets the stage for delighted hearts: "The rod and reproof give wisdom. . . . Discipline your son, and he will give you rest; he will give delight to your heart" (Prov. 29:15, 17).

Corporal punishment should be relatively infrequent and can be incrementally eliminated over time as the child develops, as other forms of correction become more effective, such as words, loss of privileges, and natural consequences.

Spankings should not injure, but should hurt—that is, administer pain, a sting. If it doesn't hurt, it doesn't deter, and the child doesn't consider it worth avoiding. Discipline inflicts pain, but not injury.

For physical punishment, I prefer using a neutral object (such as a wooden spoon)—something the child can feel, but which won't injure his body. There can be urgent exceptions when the parent's hand can be used—as when a child is biting a playmate or choking his little sister—and there's no time to fetch an implement. The child's misbehavior must be stopped *now*!

9

In the Moment

When your child misbehaves, and the moment has come for corrective discipline, you want to be ready to act *promptly and decisively* to move your child in the direction of compliance with your standards.

Know the Situation

Before correcting your child, be *certain* that correction in this situation is truly in order.

To that end, listening to your child is essential. As appropriate, provide opportunity for the child to explain. Find out if your guidelines were clear and firm.

Have you established what actually happened? You may need to ask eyewitnesses.

Is the child being truly defiant, or is he merely pushing against walls that are unsure?

Discern. For example, there's a difference between a little fidgeting and willfully aggravating those around you. Was the child blatantly disobedient, or did he simply make an honest boo-boo in spilling the milk? Distinguish between willful defiance and playfulness, between mischief and accidents. Defiance and mischief aren't the same, though they can overlap.

Are your expectations in this situation realistic? You can't expect a child to not wet his pants on a three-hour drive with no stops. Put to rest expectations of the impossible. Be realistic. Your child is a child. But he shouldn't remain childish forever. Being very young can explain trial-and-error mishaps, but it's no excuse for defiance. Don't expect too much or too little.

Strive to see the situation through the child's eyes, making any necessary adjustments in your response so the correction lands the way it's intended to land—as loving.

Especially important is being certain that you were clear and specific beforehand in defining boundaries and limits. Are you sure the child knew and understood the instructions? If she isn't complying, maybe it's because she didn't hear you, and not because of any defiance. Were the consequences of misbehavior spelled out to the child in advance? "If you do X, then Y will happen."

What If You're Uncertain?

What if you're not absolutely certain the child was defiant? Keep the following sentence handy: "I'm going to take your behavior as _____."

When it isn't clear to you whether or not the child has been naughty or rebellious, say something like this: "I'm not clear on whether you were being sassy right there. So nobody's in trouble. But if you speak to your mother in that tone again, or make that face again, I'm going to view your behavior as sassiness, and you'll receive consequences you won't enjoy."

This isn't punitive; it's clarifying. It fairly puts the child on notice. It's a wise and loving warning.

One Warning Only

Once you've definitely established that the child has violated a command or rule, which he clearly understood in this situation, then skip any further warnings. Instead, immediately apply the consequences you've set up in advance. The child has already been warned, and has defied that warning. It's time for you as the parent to act.

Your pattern should be to give only one warning. Mean what you say. Otherwise you foster more disobedience, teaching your child that the first warning means little.

As you articulate your warning, it's often good to use key questions like these:

What are you supposed to be doing?

Do you understand what you're to do?

What did I say? (Or, if the instruction came from another authority, *What did Grandma say? What did your coach say? What did your teacher say?*)

Although posed as questions, these are not an invitation for discussion. Rather, they're meant to clearly establish the child's personal responsibility and your own authority as the parent. These questions are meant to communicate this message: "I mean what I said, and if you don't start complying right now, I'll take corrective action immediately."

This confirms that your instructions were meant, and that the child has arrived at a morality juncture: his next actions will either be naughty or cooperative. This moral dimension is important for shaping the child's conscience. There is right and there is wrong, and it doesn't matter whether the child is tired or hungry or disappointed from not getting his way.

Sometimes, upon being given a directive (put your shoes on; hang up your jacket; take your dishes to the sink), a child is spurred on by the simple parental statement: "Let me see you do it." These words jump-start your child into immediate obedience.

Be Clear and Calm

In these moments, ensure you have the child's attention. "Caleb, put down your video game and look at me." Make direct eye contact, letting him know he has *your* attention. Address him calmly by name. Inspect his nonverbals for confirmation that your message is reaching those little ears.

Meanwhile, retain your own composure and self-control. Avoid a harsh tone of voice. How you speak can matter as much as what you say. Avoid sarcasm and ridicule, which are communication killers and spirit wounders. Decisive correction and gentleness go hand in hand. Your goal is not to humiliate, but to train.

Be especially concerned to control your anger or similar emotions. You may want to label those feelings: "I'm disappointed"; "I'm angry"; "I'm anxious." Such statements allow you to identify what's going on inside you, to step outside those feelings, and to preach to yourself about them, all the while modeling self-control to the child.

Express your warning to the child clearly, not vaguely:

"If you throw the truck, I'll get the rod."

(*Not:* "If you don't shape up, I'm going to get angry.")

"If you aim that Nerf gun at anyone, I'll take it away."

(*Not:* "Be careful with that thing.")

"If you continue using that tone of voice, you'll be sent to your room."

(*Not:* "Settle down!")

"When you whine, I automatically deny your request; are you whining?"

(*Not:* "Your whining drives me nuts.")

"Should you throw your toy across the living room like that? No? Then don't do that anymore."

(*Not:* "Go easy, Buster.")

"This calls for the rod" (and reach for it).

(*Not:* "Knock it off, or I'll wring your neck.")

Make your warning as simple and concrete as possible. Instead of saying, "Mommy doesn't want you to be quite so rambunctious," just say, "Sit." That's not vague or complicated.

After the Warning

If there's insufficient compliance with your warning, then immediately begin applying the correction you've established. Apply the painful consequence.

And if there *is* compliance—then reward it. Thank your child for his cooperation and good behavior. Everybody likes to be appreciated for a good job or even for a good try.

If the child cries as you administer correction, discern the difference between a sorrowful cry and an angry, demanding hissy fit. The former is to be expected and is healthy. The latter is naughty and is to be corrected after further warning.

My father could discern the difference (so can you), and when I was overdoing it with my postcorrection cry, he would interject: "Stop crying like that, or I'll give you something to cry about." Since I knew he meant it, I turned off my excessive crying. In the process, I discovered I could overrule my immature, impetuous, demanding emotions. I was awakening to the possibility that my mood is not my God. My mood isn't all-powerful, and my moody agenda need not reign over me or others.

Remember: a child can be taught to be obedient, even when he doesn't at first feel like obeying. He can be given a swift consequence that he likes even less than not getting his own way. In the moment, children don't have to like what they're required to do. The same goes for adults. Children and adults can do difficult things they don't like at the moment, and be glad later that they did.

The moment of correction may be a time to explain to your child (and to yourself) that love requires discipline.

Persist

How long must a parent insist on the child's compliance in a given situation?

Answer: Until there's no defiance, and obedience occurs.

This takes a great deal of intentional, sustained focus and commitment, especially in the early going. But is it worth it? Yes.

Ask God for the willingness to consistently respond to your child's misbehavior every time, and for as long as he keeps on with his misbehavior. Outlast him. The child may be strong-willed. Be stronger. You're not a bully when you outlast your child; you're an effective parent. That's your job.

It can be extremely draining emotionally to outlast a child's repeated resistance, whining, and tantrums, but if you don't outlast him, you'll only get more resistance and defiance in the future. If you do outlast him, it will result in benefits tomorrow and throughout the future.

When You're Wrong

What if you discover afterward that the correction you administered was not actually called for?

Parents can deceive themselves into thinking they're right, when they're dismally and destructively wrong. *We* need correction.

Humbly admit your error. Ask your child's forgiveness. Re-state belongingness, love, and commitment, then have another go at it. What great modeling it is for children to see their parents confessing, apologizing, and repenting!

After You Correct

After you've corrected your child and the punishment is over, it's important to demonstrate your affection.

While visiting a church, I sat behind a father with a three-year-old boy who began to make noise by rubbing his hand back and forth over his chair. The man swiftly, gently, firmly, and silently put his hand over the boy's hand, stopping the noise. No scowling. No histrionics.

After getting compliance, the father tenderly tussled the boy's hair. The entire operation took only a few seconds. But it was full of powerful meaning!

Following correction, it's especially important to show acceptance. Teach and renew belongingness following an infraction. "You know, Billy, your disobedience doesn't stop you from being my son or stop me from loving you, any more than my sin stops God from loving me as his child."

"You're still my daughter, Megan, and I still love you very much." Underscore your own personal responsibility before God and your accountability to him. The point of discipline is not so we can exercise brute power, but to prepare the child for responsibility and freedom.

Demonstrate safety. Gently touch the child. If she draws away from you, more time for mending the relationship may be required. If the drawing away shows defiance, the episode may not be over.

Be aware that though a child can be required to behave immediately, heart change usually takes a little longer. If the child feels wounded by the episode, it could take a little while for the storm to pass.

My experience has been that when I disciplined children most firmly, within thirty minutes or so we were on good terms again. Laughter returned. My young children and grandchildren were almost predictably sitting on my lap voluntarily within a half hour of a disciplinary episode, asking to play a game with me. And I received those invitations warmly, because I wanted to demonstrate that there were no hard feelings, that I loved them, and that the crisis was behind us. Onward we go.

A tender touch cannot only test for harbored hardness of heart, bitterness, or unresolved grievances, but also foster emotional intimacy. Oh, the ministering, healing touch of Jesus!

The postcorrection time may call for a tender debriefing. Strive toward mutual understanding as you together review and discuss what happened and why. "Megan, do you understand why a loving parent has to correct his child's naughtiness? Parents don't want the children they love to stay naughty, just like God doesn't want us to stay sinful."

Pray with your child. God will help you pray with myriad texts off the front burner of your devotional life. So keep your devotional life up to date as you press forward in the honor and awesome responsibility of parenting.

Appendix

Questions from Parents

You might feel overwhelmed by the advice offered in this book. Take a breath. Break the goal down into small steps, and take one step at a time. Find a pace to finish the race.

Meanwhile, here are my answers to some specific questions related to corrective discipline that parents have asked me.

Is there a connection between boredom and misbehavior?

One key to maintaining a young child's cooperative interest is to occasionally vary the child's activity, keeping an eye on his or her attention span. Though brevity is not king, it's a value. Within a time span, you can vary the activities every few minutes according to the child's development and interests.

Boredom kills. Variety is the proverbial spice of life. Change things around. Change the furniture, the decorations (put the kids in charge), or the order of events. Pity the child who has to be strapped in an infant seat for a long drive. Have mercy.

Know and understand each individual child; don't simply overlay an artificial "attention span" limitation on them.

Once, in order to free a mom during a women's meeting at our church, I took her eighteen-month-old daughter to my office, where she sat on my lap and fiddled with my typewriter while I worked at my desk. Amazingly, the typewriter kept her attention for a full forty-five minutes before she became disinterested. Her attention span was much longer than I would have predicted. But once she became bored with the typewriter, there was no use trying to entertain her with the keyboard any longer.

Read the child.

What if the child needing correction is not my own?

Though it's a last resort, not a first option, oust the troublemaker. Tell him, "If you can't cooperate with our reasonable rules, you can't be here." If the child is determined to persist, you must be ready to outpersist him.

For example, church workers can consider taking the offending child to sit with the parents in the grownups' class. I did that once when I was working with a group of children at church. I had to do it only once.

Is it too late to start? What if we've been practicing poor corrective habits for a long time, and now our child is a teen?

It's true that a teenager can "take you" (run away, steal the car, get pregnant, etc.). Nevertheless, it's always the right time for you to mean what you say and to follow through. If you've established a pattern of failed threats, own up to your failure, confess it as wrong (to yourself, your spouse, your God, and your teenager), and announce the turning over of a new leaf, with God's help.

You're wise to suspect that significant tightening of the enforcement of house rules is likely to meet with a strong reaction. But easing into it is disingenuous and inconsistent. So explain what you're about to do. Then do it.

Expect increased resistance prior to acceptance of the new normal. When increased rebellion happens, you may want to say that you were expecting this, but that your no still means no.

Does the responsibility to correct your children go away when they reach a certain age?

No, but *how* you go about it does change.

How young is too young?

Don't punish newborns. It's the extremely rare baby who can comprehend his offense during the first few months of life, much less make an association between an offense and some resultant punishment administered by an overstriding parent.

Let me hasten to add that children just a few months of age can begin to arch their backs in defiance of their parents, and such defiance can and *should* be met with correction.

What kind of correction? For one thing, don't allow the arched back to dictate. For another, you can hold the child firmly, without harshness, until he stops arching his back. Outlast him, so that he understands he's not in charge, and his back-arching is an unwelcome and unrewarded behavior.

You can say no to a very young child and back it up by physically restraining naughty behaviors such as biting or hitting you in the face.

Small infants—prior to learning to speak—are fully capable of discovering how to manipulate their parents. For example, they cry and cry, and you rush to pick them up. They reward you with quieting down. They didn't *need* anything—they weren't hungry, didn't have a soiled diaper, didn't have a toe uncomfortably curled inside their sock. They just want to drive the bus, and you're the bus. In the process, fussy babies are rewarded for fussing when mommies scurry to pick them up at every whimper.

Yes, there are exceptions—such as colicky babies and very sick babies. But it will do a well-fed and dry child no harm to lie safely and cry himself to sleep, which is harder on the parent than on the child. To speak this way is not advocating neglect, abuse, or harshness. Wise parents strike a balance between giving the legitimate attention that helps an infant flourish and the kind of attention that gives rise to a tiny dictator.

When a child comes to realize that the exhausting work of extended crying is simply not going to achieve his aims (getting attention, being in control, etc.), the behavior will disappear, although it may temporarily spike before it's gone. A child who's about a year old should be corrected wisely, lovingly, decisively, consistently, gently, and firmly. That may sound too general, but I want to avoid simplistic formulas.

Don't discipline a young child for failing to comply with an expectation he can't meet. Children can't grow up without spilling, for example. Spills happen. Accidents happen. But when a child clearly demonstrates that he *can* comply with a standard you want him to obey, then you can begin to hold him responsible. For example, when you know your child can say please or thank you, it's reasonable to begin expecting that child to say it.

Children can be patiently taught to obey without prematurely expecting them to behave like adults.

My teen sleeps late and won't go to church with us. Should we wake him?

If you want him to go to church (and I'm assuming you do), then yes. His sleeping is disobedience.

Does he live in your home? Then he should follow your household practices. Have you articulated the principles and benefits behind your household rules? Does he know you love him? Do you affirm him when he cooperates? Do you commend the commendable in his other behaviors? Then show the contrast of your displeasure when he oversleeps. Is he required to go to school or a job or other functions? Whatever you do to require him to go to those other functions can be applied to requiring him to go to church.

How do you reward him? If allowing him to sleep late is its own reward (from his point of view) for skipping church, then by letting him sleep you're *rewarding* him for church-skipping.

Do you model enthusiasm, faithfulness, and self-discipline in doing things *you* don't always enjoy, but believe are important in order to avoid future regret? Do you complain about going to church yourself?

How can we get our children to sleep?

In addition to the standard wisdom of monitoring sugar intake, shifting toward quieter and less rambunctious activities toward bedtime (reading books instead of dueling with light sabers), I discovered a couple of remarkably effective practices. When putting children to sleep, don't say simply, "Go to sleep," since nobody (including parents) can obey that command. When a person isn't sleepy, he isn't sleepy. Perhaps the child is simply wide awake and can't sleep. Don't put him in the impossible situation of having to obey a command he cannot obey.

Rather, say something like this: "Lie down, close your eyes, and lie still." That command can be obeyed, even if he doesn't go to sleep.

When sitting next to a child as she lies still (with your desire that she go to sleep), don't let her hands touch her face. There's something stimulating about the hand touching the face, which works against drifting off to sleep. Gently pull her hands away from her face. The hands can instead be holding a stuffed animal, or folded together, or in some other position.

You can also slowly, tenderly cover her eyes and close the lids with your fingers. Sometimes this can be done without actually touching the eyelids or eyelashes. By gently and *slowly* stroking downward between the eyebrow and the eyelash, the child's eyes will close almost involuntarily. And the result is often (not always) sleep.

How do I stop a child from climbing out of bed?

If this is an issue that's disturbing your home's peace, then to establish that peace, you must elevate this climbing-out-of-bed issue to a higher place than whatever else you're doing at the time. It's more important than watching your favorite TV program, or finishing up the dishes, or relaxing a few minutes with your feet up, or preparing yourself for bed. You've issued a command, and your first job is to make your words mean what you said.

It's not just about the child going to bed. It's about bigger things, like submitting his will to the will of an authority, learning that he's not in charge of the universe. When you persist in this, you're loving him. To think you're too busy or too tired to follow through is to make a grave and costly mistake.

Mean what you say, and consistently apply the consequence.

What about children with Attention-Deficit/Hyperactivity Disorder?

I feel a great measure of sorrow for dear friends whose children with severe learning disabilities present exhausting challenges at almost every turn. I groan with them—and with all creation—at this manifestation of the fallen world in which we live, awaiting the day when "the creation itself will be set free from its bondage to decay and obtain the freedom of the glory of the children of God" (Rom. 8:21). I earnestly ask God for breakthroughs, relief, rest, and joy. Yet God in his infinite wisdom sees fit for the problems and challenges to persist.

Children are not identical with regard to how quickly they benefit from correction. There's a continuum, from quick learners to those who are less quick. Even in cases of attention-deficit/hyperactivity disorder (ADHD) and autism, only in the most severe cases (which are rare) does the child fail to pay attention to the fact that it's painful to sit on pointy objects, and therefore, when he sits on something painful, he gets off of it. He modifies his behavior to avoid sitting on pointy objects or picking up prickly items with his fingers or staring directly into the sun.

To state the obvious, attention deficit is a deficit in attentiveness, a shortage of heedfulness. Attentiveness isn't merely a physiological capacity; it's also a character quality that can be shaped and developed, like all character qualities.

I've known some children who were deficient in attentiveness learn to not do things like poke themselves in the eye with pencils. Why don't they do such painful things? One straightforward reason is that they learn to pay *attention* to the pain produced when they're inattentive. The negative reinforcement of pain has a shaping effect on their future behaviors, and the positive reinforcement of pleasure also has a shaping effect.

Attentiveness doesn't require genius; it does require heedfulness and wakefulness. Correction awakens.

Some children have special needs, but we do them no favors by allowing their "specialness" to be a license to evade adaptation to reality and natural consequences in the world. ADHD can be an explanation for quirkiness, but it's no warrant for naughtiness.

Every child—including every ADHD child—has a spiritual nature made in the image of God. All children manifest character qualities, good or bad. Brains and hearts are involved in the decisions made by all of us, including ADHD children. Certain behaviors are clearly defiant, though it's trickier to distinguish in ADHD children, and sometimes we just don't know. But when we do know, those behaviors call for correction.

Does practicing correction guarantee there will be no prodigals?

No. In a fallen world, practicing correction well is no guarantee that compliance and obedience will be achieved. However, short of an ironclad guarantee, we do have a great measure of assurance that correction which is well-practiced, consistent, and begun early will bring fruitful and happy results. "Folly is bound up in the heart of a child, but the rod of discipline drives it *far* from him" (Prov. 22:15). Drives it far from him? Yes. But the rod must be applied wisely, consistently, and in the context of many other parenting dynamics such as affirmation, humble modeling, and other factors.

What is it that the rod drives from the child? Folly. The rod does not, and cannot, drive out the folly of unbelief, because that is a divine work. But the rod *can* drive out the folly of failing to make connections between actions and consequences.

The foolish generally don't see their own folly as folly. They need assistance in seeing it. They need awakening.

Being faithful to attempt correction doesn't by itself guarantee that the situation will be all straightened out and all parties will behave as though they're perfectly sanctified. There will be failures in your child's behavior, and there will be failures in your parenting. What will be your attitude toward such failures?

God is bigger than parental failure. When we apply his grace, he gives more.

How can I correct an attitude?

We can correct behaviors that are *manifestations* of attitudes. If it's not clear that a behavior is stemming from an unacceptable attitude, we can openly point out the behavior, and without yelling or debating or accusing the child of wrongdoing, simply state that in the future such behaviors will be considered expressions of the unacceptable attitude and will be punished accordingly.

For example, not listening can be a manifestation of self-centered preoccupation. A preoccupied person can be awakened to consider others—whether that awakening requires a tap on the shoulder, a word, a whistle, a traffic ticket, a spanking, or incarceration, depending on the context.

A pattern of interruptions can be a manifestation of pride. Quietly say, "You're interrupting," perhaps with your index fingers lifted to your lips or some other nonverbal cue. Interrupting isn't necessarily headstrong, but a *pattern* of it is, especially when the child is asked to wait before speaking, and to not interrupt.

Or consider stubbornness. Dogged determination can be a strong quality to commend, and there's a fine line between being determined and being stubborn. One evidence of stubbornness is the continual effort to have the last word. This must be curbed in our children.

Virtually all parents are acquainted with the situation in which a certain toy is completely ignored by their child until another child takes an interest in that toy. It isn't quite accurate to say that a child is automatically naughty for taking renewed interest in a toy simply because a playmate shows interest in it, any more than saying it's wrongheaded for an unbeliever to take interest in Christ Jesus when he sees his Christian neighbor enjoying Christ. But the way a child *expresses* his interest in his neighbor's toy is either bad (stealing it back) or good (joining in the play). The *expression* is the manifestation of attitude that we can address.

How can I teach my children to tell the truth?

1. Model truth personally—to your children, to the IRS, to store clerks, to God. Let your children see you correcting yourself, clarifying misrepresentations, and telling the truth when it "costs" you. Do this modeling consistently. Your whole life is modeling, and your private life will eventually and inevitably spill over into your public life. Your sins will find you out.

2. Provide verbal teaching about truth-telling. Especially emphasize that truthfulness wins future trust. To be trusted in the future, we must handle present facts truthfully. One's falsehood will forfeit his future believability. Tell your children about the boy who cried wolf.

3. Include the child in establishing the consequence for lying.

4. Express suspicion in specific unconfirmed cases, while granting the benefit of the doubt. If you don't have eyewitnesses or firm evidence, grant the benefit of the doubt. "Something

doesn't add up to me, but I'm going to proceed as though you're telling me the truth."

5. Pray for grace—the enablement to do what's right—for both you and your child. Memorize and recite Scripture together. Ask together to be filled with the Spirit. Encourage an active walk with God, underscoring his omnipresence.

I thank God for the continual reminders of my mother that God is with us wherever we go. That's good news. It's good news if you're ever telling the truth in a tight spot, and no one believes you; God knows you're telling the truth, and at the right time he'll be your vindication. It's also good news if you think you're getting away with a secret sin and covering it up with a lie, because you're already found out, which may disabuse you of kidding yourself and help you lay down any resistance you may have to God's relentless effort to produce Christlikeness in his children.

6. When a child tells the truth, praise him!

My Prayer for You

Our Father, enable this one whom you have appointed as parent to wisely identify actions and attitudes in each child that are unacceptable when weighed against clear and explicit standards. Help this parent to take prompt, decisive, effective action to joyfully move each child in the direction of respectful compliance. Yes. Amen.

General Index

Scripture Index

Also Available from Sam Crabtree

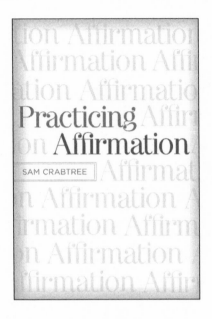

"The practice and power of affirmation will make a difference in the life of anyone, young or old. *Practicing Affirmation* will help you make a positive investment in your relationships—even when people are difficult."

BRUCE JOHNSON, President, SIM USA

"This book is an invaluable resource to the church. How do we effectively 'build each other up in the faith?' You're holding the answer in your hands!"

JONI EARECKSON TADA, Founder and CEO, Joni and Friends
International Disability Center

"I am grateful for this book—if no one else needs it, I know I do!"

NANCY DEMOSS WOLGEMUTH, author; Bible teacher; Host,
Revive Our Hearts

For more information, visit **crossway.org**.